Iben Sandahl was born in Denmark and grew up in Aarhus. She later moved to Copenhagen, where she became a teacher and licensed psychotherapist with her own private practice. She is known for her Danish parenting philosophy and her insistence on equipping parents, educators and leaders with a fundamentally new vision of what is possible in the world. Her values encompass a belief in children's rights to be their authentic selves, with a safe childhood that allows them to grow at their own pace.

Iben's main objectives are to inspire, help and support parents and professionals to ensure that new generations of children can grow up with the highest degree of social and mental health by offering alternatives to the downward spiral in happiness that is seen everywhere today. She offers lectures, workshops and counselling to parents and families, as well as public organisations and private enterprises, and her methods have been followed by thousands of families, schools, colleges, universities and organisations worldwide.

She writes for *Psychology Today* and her writing has also featured in the *Washington Post, HuffPost, The Atlantic, Quartz, The New York Times* and *Greater Good Magazine* from the Science Center at Berkley, to name just a few. She is a mother of two daughters, Ida and Julie.

www.ibensandahl.com

ALSO BY IBEN DISSING SANDAHL

The Danish Way of Parenting (Piatkus, 2016)

Play The Danish Way (Ehrhorn Hummerston, 2017)

My Tummy Hurts, Mom (Gyldendal, 2018)

Do you want to raise Happy Children? Parent the Danish Way (online course, 2019)

Empathy For Children (Erasmus+ Project: Improving the level of key Empathy competences and skills of pupils, also applied to entrepreneurship, 2021)

Iben Dissing Sandahl

The Danish Way of Raising Teens

**What the happiest people in the
world know about raising confident,
healthy teenagers with character**

PIATKUS

PIATKUS

First published in Great Britain in 2023 by Piatkus

1 3 5 7 9 10 8 6 4 2

A CIP catalogue record for this book
is available from the British Library.

ISBN 978-0-349-43573-2

Typeset in Baskerville by M Rules
Printed and bound in Great Britain by
Clays Ltd, Elcograf S.p.A

Papers used by Piatkus are from well-managed forests
and other responsible sources.

Piatkus
An imprint of
Little, Brown Book Group
Carmelite House
50 Victoria Embankment
London EC4Y 0DZ

An Hachette UK Company
www.hachette.co.uk

www.littlebrown.co.uk

To Ida and Julie

You are the most beautiful shining stars I
know, and without your love and bringing
about my shadow sides, I would not be
the person I am today. My heart is full
of gratitude for our deep relationship
and for witnessing how you have become
spirited, independent women with
character. I love you fully and wholly.

ACKNOWLEDGEMENTS

I want to thank my husband, Morten, for once again being my greatest support as I wrote this book – in this and all other matters of our life together, you always have my back. I love you. Likewise, my two beloved daughters, Ida and Julie, have been my most incredible educators in the journey to become whole. They have contributed with their input and perspectives on teenage life. They have been the source of my personal and professional wisdom and insights. Frederick Utzon Harris should be thanked in the same way. He has led me into the many nuances of the masculine side of youth life with ideas and examples, alongside loving Julie in the most beautiful and wholehearted way. My soulmate Cathrin Christensen must be given a special thank-you for all our current and significant conversations in Dyrehaven. Without these, I would not have understood my extinct stars and myself on the deep level you led me to. A special thank-you, too, to my mom and dad because I would not be who I am without them: you gave me life and essential values that have formed my life as a mother. Jillian Young, my editor, who believed and trusted in me – thank you for bringing this book alive for parents all over the world.

And, of course, all the readers and followers who inspire me with their stories deserve a heartfelt thank-you. You support me every single day, and I feel grateful for the love and encouragement sent to me, letting me know that my words make a difference in your life.

Contents

Introduction

I have known for many years that I would write this book one day, and the time is simply now.

I had a dream of communicating hope and faith for parents raising teenagers, letting everyone know that time with adolescents can be so much more than just frustration and despair.

My name is Iben Dissing Sandahl, and I am the mother of two wonderful daughters: Ida, 22, and Julie, 19. I am a trained teacher and psychotherapist who grew up in Denmark among the happiest people on earth. I have worked with children and young people all my adult life: in psychiatry, in schools, and as a family counsellor dealing with gang crime and delinquent children. For 15 years, I have been self-employed with my own therapeutic clinic, where I treat children and families locally and internationally. In addition to this, I also have a career abroad, where I convey the Danish philosophy of parenting and participate in projects that aim to promote the well-being of children and young people. I am married to Morten, and we also have an adorable dog named Vega. I had an eye-opening experience early on. It transformed my fear of raising teenagers, with all the worries and challenges, into something I looked at with curiosity and positive expectations. This I want to share with you.

Many Danes feel sceptical about the fact that Denmark has been voted the happiest country in the world by the OECD for more than 40 years. We have a realistic view of what and how reality is among ourselves, so being happiest seems a little over the top. Nevertheless, the OECD has kept voting for Denmark. Other studies suggest that we have a genetic disposition for happiness. The research shows that, the closer a nation is to the genetic make-up of Denmark, the happier that country is. Today Denmark remains in the top two, recently overtaken by Finland. There are, of course, many parameters to be taken into account when a country is categorised as the happiest, but upbringing was never considered. This amazed me, as we all come from a common foundation that forms the framework of our self-understanding, norms and values. What else but childhood and the formative years, the starting point for all of us, can we boast of creating? I can't think of much else.

In 2015 I co-wrote *The Danish Way of Parenting*, with Jessica Alexander, about why upbringing is influenced by ingrained values that make confident and capable kids who then turn into happy adults, and the cycle repeats itself. The book – available in 32 languages – points out some special areas, characterised as:

- **Play**: essential for development and well-being
- **Authenticity**: fosters trust and an 'inner compass'
- **Reframing**: helps kids cope with setbacks and look on the bright side
- **Empathy**: allows us to act with kindness towards others
- **No ultimatums**: no power struggles or resentment
- **Togetherness** (*Hygge*): a way to celebrate family time, on special occasions and every day

I was sceptical in the beginning. But I found it delightful and highly eye-opening to delve into what lay as the foundation for my childhood, looking at how my parents prioritised free-play, authenticity, and a lot of *hygge* with an empathetic and positive approach. It seemed natural to me, and for most Danes, and therefore I didn't find it different or special compared to other places in the world. Of course, I tried to outline the more-or-less obvious differences. I was overwhelmed by the tremendously positive feedback from gracious parents, grandparents and educators all over the world, something that I could have never imagined. Everywhere I came to lecture about the Danish parenting philosophy, for conferences, summits or in educational organisations, I had the privilege to meet people who showed up to hear me. I slowly became convinced that even though Denmark is not a utopia, we must be doing something right. I started to understand the differences, and my process of really embracing what I had conceptualised had begun.

I am at a stage now where I can speak freely from my

heart, sharing the stories of my private life as a child, a teenager, an adult, spouse, mother and professional. I share my knowledge with humility and the understanding that I have become an example of Danish parenting values, which I will always carry with respect. My biggest vision is to make the world a better place. I want to bring positivity and love into the lives of all children and let them know that they are loved exactly as they are, and that is achieved through helping adults be more present to the needs of children. This is why I am reaching out to parents, caregivers and institutions, as the entire process embodies my purpose most beautifully that way.

Beliefs

Many parents believe that there's nothing more they can do once they have a teenager in their household – by then it's somehow out of their hands and they cannot make an impact on them any more. In general terms, in the media and among adults, and mostly ingrained in our narratives and affirmed in our culture, I think the terminology around teenagers has a negative and judgemental character. Parents who have a challenging relationship with their teens are convinced that bad behaviour is the teen doing something against them personally.

When children are small, they learn norms, rules and values on our terms; what we bring with us of traditions and behaviour, and what we value and enjoy in life. When they become teenagers, they need to find their own identity on their own terms. If teens are to become responsible adults, they need to know which of our rules, norms and values they can adopt as their own. This requires everything to be considered, chewed on and spat out. Needless to say, this does not always look like our idea of good behaviour. So, our teens' behaviour is not always about doing something against our wishes, but about becoming themselves, exactly who they truly are.

In Danish we use terms to describe our teenager or our neighbour's teenager such as they are inaccessible, that they only do what they want, that they are becoming more and more independent and 'frontier seeking'. They are too lazy and unmotivated. They have no respect for authorities, and they drink or smoke too much, and lack control in terms of their lives. I think these are quite rough labels to put on anyone, especially while still growing up and learning about life. Since they are evolving and still very impressionable it is essential for us to begin to find new ways of looking at them and talking about and with them. Words matter and can have a significant influence on what they believe about themselves. We want to help them become strong and resilient young adults. Yet, instead, we point fingers at them and label them negatively. It is neither fair nor reasonable because they are, at least in part, relating and behaving in ways that have been shown them by their parents or guardians at home.

Some suggest that you can sit back, put your feet up, and feel satisfied when becoming a teen parent. At that point, most of the work has been done. To this, I agree and disagree. I fully understand that teenagers detach themselves from us and test rules, values and boundaries – this is only healthy and necessary to become independent. In that case, it is OK for us to relax on the couch. I would never want my girls to be a carbon copy of me. That, in my optics, would be skipping an essential part of their development. It is a vital time for them, and therefore we must let go of the control that causes us to meddle in everything to make ourselves feel somewhat safe, so they can find out who they are themselves. Because that is what this is all about. Our needs often seem more important than theirs.

I disagree about the part that we should leave them to get on with it on their own, as they need our attention, guidance and support continuously; we just have to do it in a new manner. The thing is that teenagers don't yet know in which direction they are going. They will make mistakes and will experience sorrow and ups and downs, and for all that they will definitely still need us to be around and to be their safe zone.

That is why we can't just let go. We continue to be important background figures, ready to grab and support them when they are searching and trying to find and become themselves; I wouldn't say that this is needed more than ever, but at least as much as earlier in their life. It is a misunderstanding, in my opinion, that they do not require our attention as they start to enter adolescence. They need you to be their rock when the ground feels quite shaky, and that is when you will need to show and tell them: 'I am here for you. You will be fine. Actually, you are learning something.' They need you to mirror what is important and valuable to you with a calmness that gives them strength and space to take ownership of their own choices and decisions. If you leave them all on their own during these vulnerable years in their life, you risk losing them forever – they need you, and they need to feel closely connected to you. Not dependent on you, but with you around if there is a need for care and support.

My perspective

When I myself became a mother, I was not initially aware of my wish to raise my daughters differently to how I was raised. In so many ways, I had a good childhood, in a happy, healthy and secure environment filled with love and with parents who were present. But there were some bumps from time to time. These were times when I didn't feel loved. To this day I still remember feeling hurt and inadequate. I have been on an inner journey as far back as I can remember, working on my mental health. I have been dedicated to developing strategies and attending counselling. When I became a mother, motherhood invited me to delve deeper into the path of looking inward to become the best possible mother to my daughters.

It's one thing to decide that we want to do things differently from our parents; it's quite another to act on that consciously. One does not necessarily follow the other. Triggers, projections and irritations tend to show up in the most unexpected ways. We blame or shame our kids before we even have time to think about it. Our body recognises something that makes us feel triggered – often some totally unconscious wounds where we may have felt unloved, and suppressed feelings arise. We would be robots if we did not experience this occasionally. I recalled repeatedly how it felt for me when I was a child and a teenager. I saw all the times and small instances where I didn't feel seen or recognised for who I am. I wanted to be certain that my daughters were not growing up having the same experiences and dealing with the same emotions that I had to deal with, and therefore, I decided to handle many things in a different manner.

I was helped through this process by remembering some good advice given to me by a colleague many years ago: '*Do not worry! It will be good and exciting. Think about how enriching it will be to see some of the tools that you have put into parenting be unfolded and utilised by your teens as they make them their own. Enjoy the ride.*'

My underlying fear about being a mother to teens changed immediately. I put on a new pair of glasses, which has forever changed my approach and ability to see and listen to children and teens. Because – what is there to fear? Not that there will not be any more challenges or challenging times. Of course they will always be there, because that is the gift of life. But if your desire to talk with and spend time with your teenager comes from a balanced and healthy place within you, then there are plenty of reasons to let go of some of your concerns. And the good news is that many of your concerns might actually never arise.

Tween or Teen

The definition of a teenager is straightforward: a teenager is a person between 13 and 19 years old. The description of tweens is a little less clearly defined. To my understanding, there is no official tween definition. Tweens are believed to go through their own changes and transitions, just as teens do. This tween journey begins at slightly varying ages, most often between the ages of 8 and 12 years old. They will increasingly start to develop independence, individuality and maturity, and gradually will behave more like a typical teenager. I think tweens have a lot in common with Peter Pan. He felt plenty of pressure from his surroundings to be an 'adult', but deep down was neither comfortable with the idea nor ready for it.

In Denmark, the word 'pre-teens' is usually applied a little ironically, to illustrate that our children have started not listening to our directions and are starting to behave more rebelliously. Tweens is not a term used here as such. I have chosen not to distinguish clearly between a teenager, tween, or pre-teenager in this book. My points are aimed at parents who experience general developmental and psychological changes in their children as they move towards adolescence. Personally, I have never focused too much on age. Since many children go into puberty long before the age of 13 today, I would like to reach out to the parents who understand my parenting starting point as a way of living, rather than a point-by-point guidebook.

With this book

What has always driven me, in everything I do, is the gift of having access to new knowledge. I am curious and I love to read and study. I have discovered that this is my inner vision. Every book, course, speech, or project I have touched has made me grow a little more, into a better and more balanced version of me. Of course, I am still a work in progress, but I sense that my journey of becoming whole as a human being is moving forward. Those who have read my books, attended my member page or taken my online course will notice that my personal stories capture this adventure quite well. I simply can't write about anything that I haven't experienced. This is exactly why my book about raising happy teenagers is here now. Now my teenagers are growing into becoming beautiful grown-ups. I have been there myself, experienced the challenges and the advantages firsthand, and I am proud and thankful to be able to say that I have an exquisite bond with both of my daughters.

I may use gender-specific terms. This is not an expression of disrespect to anyone. I do not assume that everyone can recognise themselves as a specific gender. So, in general terms I aim to use 'teen', 'child', or 'adolescent'. Likewise, it is important to point out that this book is not an expression of therapy or professional family counselling. If you have problems that require treatment, you must seek professional help in the right places. As for this book, I want to share my own life story, but even more important, I want to give you an insight into how

Danish parents deal with the many facets of being a parent to teenagers – the Danish way – raising happy, autonomous and confident human beings with character.

The six aspects of Danish parenting from my co-authored first book are re-examined in relation to life with teenagers in this book. In addition, four new ones have been added, which are now relevant to describe in this exciting phase from child to adult. These are:

- **Trust** – The building block for a happier and more worry-free life
- **Formation** – How to grow into an educated and insightful human being with sufficient autonomy
- **Uniqueness** – Learning to love and identify the 'me'
- **Freedom with responsibility** – An insight into the Danes' alcohol culture

I look forward to sharing life with teenagers and the beautiful, laborious and rewarding experiences that light up our life with you.

With love and gratitude,
Iben Dissing Sandahl

CHAPTER 1

Authenticity

THE TRANSITION PHASE

Teenage years are full of changes that reveal the vulnerable, authentic self. It is a sensitive time when our teens seek peace and inner balance but seldom get there; these goals tend to be unrealistic considering what is happening within them while at the same time facing a diverse world of uncertainty and high expectations. Suppose we focus on what our teenagers tell us through their behaviour and honestly and pragmatically understand what is happening within ourselves too. In that case, we can better support them in this phase, lower our and our teens' expectations and possibly grow even more as parents and let them truly flourish.

> Authenticity is feeling connected to your true self and having the capacity to connect on a deeper level with other people. Authenticity is following the beliefs or values that will make your life blossom.

A new phase

It is common for girls to go into puberty around 10 years old, while for boys it's around 11 or 12 years old. This can vary and is, among other things, also genetically determined. There is not yet much knowledge about how the body knows it is time. But what is evident is that the first signals come from the brain. The pituitary gland (a small gland the size of a pea that sits behind the eyes) sends hormones via the bloodstream down to the ovaries or testicles and stimulates the sex hormones oestrogen and testosterone – also known as the female and male sex hormones. In girls, it initially causes the breasts and uterus to grow. Likewise the first sign of puberty in boys is seen by their testicles growing. Of course, there are always a few instances of variation. Both boys and girls get pubic hair and sweat odour due to increased testosterone production. Girls get a more feminine fat distribution, where the fat accumulates around the hips. They also gain increased muscle mass due to testosterone, but not to the same extent as boys, whose voices also begin to transition. It is literally here that children's bodies become adults.

It is also during this period that greater differences emerge. Some grow tall; others remain short. Some get big breasts while others don't. Some produce a lot of hair growth while others only a little. Some feel comfortable in their bodies; others do not. It is undoubtedly an exposed time that causes uncertainty and induces self-criticism in most teenagers.

There is much that implies that more children are entering puberty earlier than before. Precocious puberty, as it is called, means that some girls begin menstruation as young as the age of eight. Some boys begin puberty as early as around nine years old. There are several theories as to why this happens, pointing to obesity, unhealthy lifestyles, diseases, chemicals in the environment, and the like. Undoubtedly, this is worrisome, as childhood is significantly shortened, thereby reducing the crucial time to prepare for the many challenges that adolescence brings.

Step in and step out

Teenagers are more upfront, requiring more knowledge and dialogue about sexuality, identity and emotions today than when I was a teenager. It has become more common to talk about bodies, feelings and boundaries. That is positive, but I find that insecurities and the most vulnerable thoughts remain an inner dialogue despite a greater openness to many other things. 'Am I beautiful enough?' 'Am I like the others?' 'Why is only one breast growing?' 'When do I know if I am ready to do "it"?' 'How can I live up to what I have seen on porn videos?'

Although anyone can google these and many more questions, there is no guarantee a healthy sorting process will influnce the answers your teenagers are presented with. The internet can often confuse and increase doubt and raise unreasonable expectations that can harm more than help.

I remember one of my daughters' friends, about ten years ago, was searching online for a particular store in the nearby mall. The store traded in teenage clothes and was called Bad Girls. Today, we know that many risqué pictures and videos will appear if you search for 'Bad Girls' online. The poor girl got terrified, and the school and parents did a lot to inform everyone about valuable guidelines on the internet as a consequence of this.

The internet is like a buffet where everyone can taste a little of everything without knowing the recipes and ingredients. You only see the perfect bodies, the big muscles, or happy and carefree lives without knowing the depths, the shadows, or the lights that have gone out inside.

There are good and bad things in all this. This is a stage of your teenager's life where they try to fit in and find themselves. The overwhelming and unfiltered amount of data on the internet that your teen has to deal with can be a little unnerving, however.

Therefore, your role in setting some directions for their choices is crucial, as their compass hasn't found north, south, east, or west yet. As much as they need to find their own path in life, they also need someone to set up a framework of sound morals and expectations.

I have always been told that I am very transparent in what I believe in and what I do not. Sometimes I may have sounded a little too bombastic or even moralistic. I have indeed stepped on people's toes unintentionally. Nevertheless, I have always relied on my inner moral compass, and it has guided me through life. I am sure that in addition to my particular personality, my compass is also influenced by my father's and mother's stories, their ways of being, and the clarity that they have shown me in how good attitudes and ethics are lived out – as well as the stars that they let sparkle in me.

I have an inner conflict with myself sometimes. I do not want to moralise or point fingers when speaking with my daughters, because I strongly believe that they need to encounter life and get some experiences on their own; me not knowing what path they will choose. So I keep my mouth shut, or just say a little and hope they will feel there is a family code of ethics and values to lean on, while still getting the freedom to form what is meaningful and important to them.

This balance can be a challenge. I am conscious of how easily my emotions are provoked by right and wrong. So much of the calibration of my nervous system rests on feeling like I can predict and know something about what's coming. I want to take responsibility for the situation. So I have to focus hard on embracing who they are at that specific time – and a deep state of lightness when I do not know comes over me. At once, I feel only love and compassion for how they are trying to master life so openly and authentically. Maybe they won't use me, and will find answers online or through friends. Or perhaps they find security at home and dare to ask the questions that are hard to ask. It is probably a mix, but I can help them choose by setting a healthy standard at home.

Communicating

I believe in having an honest and nonjudgemental dialogue with my children and that it is possible to support and help them through this sensitive period of their lives. Sometimes I have failed and jumped on them, metaphorically speaking, which hurts to admit, but my intentions have never been bad. I have always tried to meet them with curiosity and with a great deal of acceptance. In particular, aiming to engage in their lives and speak with them with mutual respect about the normality of all the many thoughts and considerations they may carry around. But also being ready to listen when they need to talk. Sometimes it works; other times, it doesn't.

For many years when Ida had just become a teenager she came to me after she went to bed. She crawled under the blanket and asked all the questions she needed answers to so that she could get peace of mind and fall asleep. They were big questions about faith, God, death, love, jealousy, anger, dreams, budding sexual thoughts, body changes – everything she had picked up from her inner and outer life that mattered to who she was turning out to be. I listened and kept my focus on what caused her thoughts and what feelings she brought into the conversation. Sometimes she needed answers or perspective to understand. Other times, she needed the reassurance that she was absolutely normal and there was no need to be worried.

That time was something special. We connected, unconditionally, and I felt more than grateful for the meaningful thoughts she shared with me. I always hugged and welcomed her even though she should have been asleep at the time, but something bigger was astir and the enormous trust she showed me made my heart melt. The gift was that she got clarification in the safest place she could ever find, and I knew I was making a significant difference for her.

I do not really recall that when I was a teenager there were any formal or constructed conversations with my mother or father to discuss or talk deeply about what happened to my body or mind while becoming a full-blown teenager. They taught me by example and when something came up naturally. I remember that I occasionally went to my father and asked about tangible things like pregnancy, abortion, contraception and puberty in general. He listened and answered my questions soberly and concretely and never indicated that he thought it was strange or that my questions made him laugh inwardly. As an adult, I have often thought about how important it was to me that I was taken seriously and not humiliated or teased for any naive or embarrassing questions I had. I remember those talks because of his kind and caring way of being with me. I wanted to pass on the same kind of space to my own children. My mother had the same approach, and I also shared a great deal of intimacy with her.

Talking about emotions, body and boundaries with someone trustworthy reduces doubt and insecurity and strengthens self-esteem in your teenager in a safe and secure environment. It normalises what needs to be normalised. Since what is 'normal' can always be debated, everyone can fit into that box, isn't that lovely?

If just the thought of these conversations coming up makes

you feel uncomfortable, consider them something very natural and necessary for your teen's development. Like when you patiently help with a maths assignment or listen to their fear of walking in the dark. Your teen will copy your way of coping with this, and if you embrace it authentically in the same way you did when you nurtured them when they cried when they were little – with care, presence and a bit of perspective – you will do fine. Omitting your own experiences and anecdotes can help your teen be more open about what to tell you, when they do not have to imagine you in various awkward situations. Use examples from other people or distant friends, and let your teen know that they have no obligation to tell you about anything they don't want to. Respecting their boundaries is always a priority; while reflecting on why this isn't a natural matter for you to talk about – if it isn't – may give you even more wisdom in your parental role. We all have different stories and values, and finding your own authentic path is valuable and important.

I am happy but also sad

Many of you will inevitably recognise that your teenagers' moods change and become more volatile. They encounter a whole new world when they experience the wave of emotions that wash over them due to altered hormones in their body. Dangling between the dependency of childhood and the responsibilities of adulthood as they are, these mood swings can be challenging to handle. Mood swings take place for all teens and are an innate part of growing up. It is only one period for teenage boys, while girls can live with mood swings much of their lives due to their menstrual cycles. As teens get older they get a better grip on their capacity to control their emotions. Conflicts simmer down and they generally learn more adaptive ways to deal with their tempers.

The reason for mood swings is to be found in the brain. It undergoes a significant rewiring twice in life, in the first years of life and again during puberty. After your baby is born, myelination (basically a process of nerve insulation) occurs in the posterior areas of the brain that are responsible for sensing and movement. After a year, your baby can start walking and standing. During puberty there is a development of this insulation and a branching of the nerves of the frontal lobes of the brain, which represent your teenager's cognitive abilities, empathy and consciousness. The brain is simply being rebuilt, and lots of new connections are emerging in these areas that enable your teenager to better put themselves in the place of others. The maturation of the brain does not mean that the teen at puberty just suddenly becomes more empathetic. In fact, it can be extra tricky for them to empathise with others because so much is changing. This emotional development isn't finished until girls reach around the age of 20, while for boys it is about 22. Young men, in particular, tend to underestimate risks and make some crazy judgements while being utterly fearless. Much of the reason for this is because the brain is simply not fully developed yet.

Dealing with mood swings can be difficult for the teenager – and for you as a parent. Conflicts sometimes arise and they are magnified by mood swings. However, the crucial point is how you handle the situation when your teen suddenly goes from laughing to crying or shouting to silence. Remind yourself of the 90-second chemical process that happens in your teen's body (after that, any remaining emotional response is simply the teen choosing, usually unconsiously, to stay in that emotional loop). Something happens that may only be sensed unconsciously and chemicals are flushed through their bodies, putting them on high alert. It takes less than 90 seconds for those chemicals to totally flush out of the body. This means that for 90 seconds, your teen can watch the process happening, they can feel it happening, and then they can watch it go away. After that, if they continue to feel fear, anger, frustration, or whatever, you can help your teen look at the thoughts they're having that are restimulating the brain circuitry that results in them having this physiological response over and over again. Besides that, the best approach for you is to remain calm, composed and patient when inter-acting with your moody teen. Their nervous system will sync with yours. Listen openly to their feelings and offer solutions or alternative interpretations, if they are open to that.

Your teens' emotional changes are expressed to a greater or lesser degree, depending on how much space they have to be themselves in the family. Suppose you are close and take an interest in their daily tasks, challenges and victories. In that case, it is easier to decode their condition and support them emotionally. It will inevitably release some stored emotional pressure they may have and thereby minimise some of their mood swings.

I never had many mood swings myself. I have not really experienced my daughters having significant mood swings either. Occasionally one of them left the dining table when discussing issues of the day, went to their room, cried, or felt unfairly treated. My husband and I allowed them to 'let off steam' and find some peace before one of us knocked on their door and was invited in. No child, teenager, or adult can talk sensibly when they are emotionally upset. Therefore, when I was the one who reached out to them, I offered to sit a little by their side without talking, if they felt OK with that. If they asked me to leave the room instead, I did. I made myself available but accepted their rejection, knowing they would come to me when they were ready. I never scolded or blamed them for their emotional outbursts. I empathised with them. When they were prepared to talk about what caused their reaction, I asked curiously with open questions. We always found each other again, without any dramatic scenes. I think it helped them to allow their feelings to show when they popped up. It also taught them to self-regulate and regain their emotional state on their own. This is essential, as they will have to deal with emotional outbursts and hurt feelings many times in their lives. As you know, they won't always have us around!

Spinning thoughts

One observation I have often made in my work with adolescents is that they describe having 'spinning thoughts'. This is not an unknown phenomenon but rather something many of us have had to deal with at some point in our lives. Teens often assume that unrelenting and racing thoughts are just the way the mind works sometimes. They do not necessarily see a correlation between the way their thoughts are manifesting themselves and the problems they are asking me to help them with. But spinning thoughts are not only symptoms of their problems. They are also a problem in themselves. I see a connection to whatever is challenging my clients and causing stress, sadness, fear, or loneliness. When teens are stressed, negative thoughts and speculations typically flow in a never-ending stream.

Just when my own daughter became a teenager she went through a period where she couldn't sleep. She struggled with spinning thoughts. No matter which technique I came up with, it only soothed her thoughts for a little while. Usually she would fall asleep but the spinning thoughts came back the next day. She adopted a lot of the things I suggested to her. She tried deep breaths, counting to 100, listening to raindrops or audiobooks. Often I also lay by her side so that the warmth of my body calmed her body. That period of her early teens taught her to take some conscious breaks during the day. In these breaks she would completely relax and sometimes meditate so that her body and mind could calm down.

You see, the mind is fascinating. Thought waves arise and subside all the time. The mind has its own rhythm and is self-conscious, even though we are unaware of many things that happen unconsciously. According to cognitive neuroscientists, we are conscious of only about 5 per cent of our cognitive activity; most decisions, actions, emotions and behaviour depend on the 95 per cent of brain activity that is beyond our conscious awareness. The latest research into the human brain suggests that the average person will typically have more than 6,000 thoughts in a single day, followed by the thousands of associations that follow a thought. This statistic comes from a team of psychology experts at Queen's University in Ontario, Canada. They developed a previously unknown way to detect when one thought ends and another begins. Of the more than 6,000 thoughts a day, 80 per cent were negative, and 95 per cent were repetitions of precisely the same thoughts as before.

There was another interesting study at Cornell University. First, scientists found that 85 per cent of what you worry about never happens. Second, with the 15 per cent of worries that did happen, 79 per cent of the subjects discovered that either they could handle the difficulty better than expected or that it taught them a lesson worth learning. The study concluded that 79 per cent of your worries are baseless and result from an unfoundedly pessimistic perception. It would seem that the subconscious mind's default position is to worry. But the science is clear – worrying is a waste of time. These baseless worries are a major source of stress and tension, and a cause of exhaustion, not only for the mind but also for the physical body. 'I've had a lot of worries in my life, most of which never happened', as Mark Twain put it. Or, as my daughter learnt from the guide on a trip down the Zambeze River at Victoria Falls in Africa: 'It's easy, like a Sunday morning.' His words instilled such a lightness and carefree spirit that it settled deep within her. It was a special and important moment, and she uses his positive approach to life to this day.

Teenagers are struggling to come to terms with not being children any more and not being adults just yet. They are trying to find their own way and their own identity in the process. There are expectations on them from every side and they have great expectations of their own. It's very hard, if not impossible to live up to so much. And as if that isn't difficult enough in itself, teenagers are subjected to a kaleidoscopic amount of information and stimuli every day. The advantages of the internet and all its communication platforms are obvious. The downside is that it can result in cognitive overload and further exacerbate whatever troubles them. No wonder teenagers worry. They have a lot on their minds. Your job is to help them however you can, by being close to them, recognising their state of mind, helping them find moments of peace during their day, and seeing if they seem emotionally fragile or stressed. You should not be overly worried as hectic times come and go. But you can teach your teen to take warning signs seriously. Symptoms like headaches, abdominal pain, mood swings, or difficulty concentrating should not be ignored. You should also help them understand spinning thoughts and where they come from. Let them know that their mind and body are theirs to take care of and that it is important to pay attention when a red light starts flashing.

There is so much wisdom to find; remember that an authentic life contains tough times but can give valuable insight for the future. After all, we connect in the cracks and scratches of being human.

Boundaries

How does authenticity look in your actions? People always tell me that I am very authentic and that they feel my presence intensely. Sometimes I wonder if the opposite of being authentic is being fake, shallow, detached, or something in between, but I am sure there are many distinctions. For me, being authentic is being just the person I am – no more nor less, but with a sky with as many sparkling stars as possible. I strive to find a balance between being true to who I am and what society and my surroundings expect from me, and I find integrity is key. If I have a reasonable balance between what I am saying, what I believe in and what I am doing, I feel authentic. I attempt to have my own opinion and the courage to stand by that opinion – always with the will to do the right thing without anyone having to monitor it. These elements are significant when listening to my gut feeling when I set boundaries for myself or what I accept my girls may and may not do.

When I was in my early twenties, I had a great desire to travel and experience other cultures. There was no one else around me who felt the same way, so I ended up travelling almost seven months around Asia all by myself. One time, I landed at Kathmandu airport in Nepal late at night without any definite plans. When I had to get transport from the airport into the city, there were no official taxi or bus options. On the other hand, there were probably about 15–20 Nepalese men all hanging over a railing and offering a lift in their old rusty cars. But who should I choose? What became clear to me throughout my journey around Asia was that when I dared to register everything my body told me according to my integrity, I chose well and discovered my boundaries. When travelling alone, I depended on my gut feelings and made choices that did not conflict with my values. I was vulnerable, alone, and receptive to the world's influences. Therefore, it became ever more important to find my boundaries to travel safely alone and in good health. That doesn't always mean that your boundaries are not exceeded, unfortunately, but knowing your boundaries is something else.

On my trip around the world, I would have a back massage – a natural thing for anyone who visited this country – and I was guided to a sinewy little man. With strong hands, he started massaging my back and moved around me as he switched sides. Suddenly I feel something bumping into one hip as he stood there. I register it but think it must be his stomach that hit my side. It happens again, and I understand that it is his erect penis. I get up promptly, take my blouse, and angrily say, 'NO! What are you doing?' and run out of the establishment. I was so embarrassed that it could happen to me. I blamed myself for my naivety, even though I knew I had not been able to foresee what had happened. But I did not share it with anyone because I was ashamed. The good thing is that I responded to my boundaries, even though it was an awful, boundary-violating experience. Sometime later I changed my blaming and shameful thoughts towards myself into thoughts of strength and pride for being able to fight for my 'survival'.

Being authentic is about knowing yourself, and is what transcends your negative thoughts, bad habits and fears, moving in a more positive direction in a common union of the intellect and the heart. When you can say either yes or no to something and respect your point of view and values, you recognise your true boundaries. You will radiate a balance and determination that shows respect and authority. It gives meaning and strength, and your teenagers will adopt it into their lives as they sense it strongly within you.

Teenagers need boundaries set by us. When we set boundaries, we create a predictable environment that means our teens know what will happen. They need to be with someone who dares to be an adult. Someone who can express what is right and wrong (for them, and the family). They need you to step into character and show who is in charge, while still keeping an open mind to the fact that it's possible to do well even if you are disagreeing about the result.

We already live in a world with boundaries that must not be exceeded, so we know the drill; for example, there are many rules we must follow when driving. The same is true at school or in the workplace, where we feel comfortable navigating within these clear boundaries. That's a good reminder that there also need to be some boundaries to thrive together in a safe family. We are the ones who set them, and we must not let our teens down in the name of love.

Today, as I see it, there is a lot of misunderstanding about roles. Far too many parents pass on too much responsibility to their children: 'What do you think we should do this weekend?' 'What do you want for breakfast?' 'Where do you want us to go on holiday?' Furthermore, we let them tell us when we are 'too much', and we adjust. We over-assist them and clean their rooms when they don't get it done. It is easier because then we avoid confrontations and can maintain a good atmosphere, when we have low expectations. We ignore our boundaries and the joint agreements we made for the sake of peace. But it is a misunderstanding of 'eye-level' parenting. Being their ally isn't the goal; you are not their friend. You are their parent – their active adult decision-maker, whom they need to rely on.

A conscious and gentle parent *is* a parent who can set boundaries and dare to say them out loud; a parent who can establish a clear framework for values and norms in the family but at the same time can enter into a dialogue with the teenager if something feels unfair to them. Setting boundaries is not about being stubborn in your beliefs but in being an unambiguous, good-enough parent that your teen can lean on confidently.

If you let go too much of the responsibility you have been given, or do not spend energy getting to know your own boundaries, then you run the risk of doing your teen a dis-service. In most cases, they will be happy with the lenient or vague answer you give them, 'I don't know. What do you think?' Still, deep down, they would rather have some clear boundaries that they can relate to – even if it might lead to conflicts here and there: 'In this family, your father and I know what is best for you. It does not mean that we don't want to listen to you and take your thoughts into consideration, but when we say no, we mean no.' In the long run, you will get a teenager who knows the boundaries they must respect and who won't be afraid of confrontations, but rather will see them as something that must be resolved with mutual respect.

When boundaries are crossed, the internal nervous system has three ways to react: fight, flight, or freeze. These vary depending on what boundary has been crossed, who does it, and whether your stress and discomfort are high or low. The foundation for your understanding of the world and the people in it was laid in your early teens and before. Maybe your experience was that your parents reacted aggressively when you asked clarifying questions, were curious, or asserted yourself. You learnt quickly to take a milder approach and give in to your parents because they were the ones you were fully dependent on. Or, maybe you learnt to freeze rather than react, because it felt safer not to run away from the situation nor to engage in confrontation. You will, without any doubt, have developed a strategy that has worked for you. Perhaps you even mirrored, through repeated observations, your parents, thereby learning to use aggression or assault when you felt threatened. Maybe your teens are learning it from you right now?

Fight, flight, or *freeze* are automatic physiological reactions to protect you from dangers. They are a stress response that helps you react to perceived threats, real or imagined. This response instantly causes hormonal and physiological changes that allow you to act quickly so you can protect yourself. It is a survival instinct that your ancient ancestors developed many years ago. Fight-or-flight is an active defence response where you fight or flee. Freezing is fight-or-flight on hold, where you further prepare to protect yourself – as when mice in test trials doze when they have no escape options. It is also called 'reactive immobility' or 'attentive immobility'. It involves similar physiological changes, but instead, you stay completely still and get ready for the next move. This state is most often when trauma is stored in the brain because the synapses do not achieve 'redemption' by an active action. Instead, they shut down and maintain an emotional resignation that can be reactivated if events evoke the same emotions or memories, when 'survival' was only about freezing, not acting. Fight-flight-freeze isn't a conscious decision. It is an automatic reaction, so it is very difficult to control.

There is a fourth reaction, not known by many. The *fawn* response involves immediately moving to please a person to avoid conflict. This is often a response developed in child-hood, where a parent or a significant authority figure is the aggressor. You go into a fawn-like response to avoid being hurt by being a pleaser. In other words, you pre-emptively try to appease the offender by agreeing, answering what you know your parent wants to hear, or by ignoring your personal feelings and desires and doing anything and everything to prevent the assault. Over time, this fawn response becomes a pattern, and this pattern carries over into your adult life with your children, teens, spouse and relatives, as well as in professional and personal interactions.

I juggle between two different reactions. When my limits are crossed on a deep emotional level, I freeze. I close down emotionally because an old inner voice reminds my nervous system that it works best for me to survive. On the other hand, I go into fight mode if I am not personally and emotionally involved but experience injustice, such as children being poorly treated or someone breaking the rules to gain an unfair advantage. I jump straight into the hornets' nest and don't worry about putting myself in jeopardy. Thinking logically where there is danger is not always possible.

To activate the fight, flight, freeze, or fawn response a stress reaction of some kind must be ignited, and this can happen in many ways: verbally, mentally, and physically. Imagine being out walking with your teenager late one night, and you suddenly spot someone standing behind a dark corner looking at you. You did not expect this, and the person moves in the dark towards you. How do you react? Do you want to fight with the stranger? Want to freeze or not know what to do? Will you run as fast as you can and hope your teen keeps up? Or numb out? What if your teenager is talking to you in a way that crosses your boundaries and awakens the same four reactions, but you would like to respond in a better and healthier manner? Then what reaction would be an alternative? What if you come to the realisation that you repeat an old pattern where your boundaries have been crossed countless times and have hurt you deeply, and you now acknowledge that you are repeating the same behaviour towards your teen with scolding or ultimatums that just teaches your teen's nervous system to react in turn. How can you change your behaviour to respect their boundaries and ensure that their automatic physiological reaction doesn't activate?

With much of what is in this book, your gaze must be turned inward to create the change you desire. It is what it is, but you can work on changing what you do not admire. It is not easy, but you risk getting a rebellious teenager if you don't somehow find a suitable way to do this. A kind way of reading your own patterns and those you are about to repeat with your teen. Not that rebellion is always bad; it is often necessary to create distance to allow a full liberation of who you are.

I find my reactions and patterns are at varying levels. Some are easier to look at and change, while others are so deeply ingrained in my DNA that they are hard to even spot. Anyone who knows me and sees me from the outside will no doubt say that I am a fighter – but I shut down and know I can take care of myself on my own! The point is that I do not want to, and if I had not identified that part of me, I could not tell those around me that I need them. They must listen to me and respect me if I feel they cross my boundaries.

I also do not want my daughters to adopt that reaction; to let others treat them in a way that they have to accept and freeze their emotions to 'survive'. Sure, as babies, we depend on our parents or caregivers to survive. Not so with teenagers or adults. Therefore, it is healthy to look at what the past has taught us.

You can begin to reflect on what triggers you, what you expect of others, or what you fear about those around you. Once you start to process this emotionally, you can move on from it and turn on star after star within you again.

Always respect one word

So, I believe that setting boundaries is essential. Be aware when your limits are exceeded. Do not point fingers, but explain why and when your boundaries are crossed, if that happens. Ask about your teen's limits informally and curiously. Not everyone knows them, but often they do know what they dislike. A conversation about boundaries can confirm to them that it is OK to feel the way they feel. In this transitional phase, boundaries, integrity and values may be strange and foreign concepts, but they need to find theirs. However, an important boundary for everyone is learning and respecting, as early in life as possible, the word 'NO'. It is pretty simple, yet so enormously important to be able to say and practise.

CHAPTER 2

Reframing

THE STARS WITHIN

Reframing means to change an imagined or emotional viewpoint about how a situation is experienced and view it differently. Reframing is about redefining negative and inhibitory beliefs, changing them into positive and supportive statements.

Have you ever thought about the extreme and unconditional love you feel when you hold your little newborn in your hands, and all your love and attention is directed wholeheartedly towards the little human being who is absolutely dependent on you? Nothing feels more terrifying and amazing at the same time, for your love is infinite and everlasting. Reality can, of course, look variegated, depending on the circumstances of the individual family, but the spontaneous joy and unconditional love apply to everyone if nothing else overshadows their happiness.

There is simply no greater and more overwhelming sense of love for those of you who have experienced that. You enter a new and vulnerable world while praising, cheering, laughing and acknowledging each little hiccup, smile, tear, attempt to eat, fart, movement, or emotional outburst, while at the same time you set your own needs on hold. You allow and welcome everything, and your baby gets your full attention. Every small step of acquiring skills in learning to be in the world is met with wonder and enthusiasm. You rejoice inside for everything presented to you, and you see your child as perfect in every possible way.

It's all about survival

I have always been fascinated by the starry sky at night. I want you to imagine looking up at the sky on a beautiful, clear, frosty night. The sky is dark and the stars shine, twinkling down as you stand there looking at the infinite universe with all its many shining stars. It is right in front of you in its full splendour, beautiful and complete, and you have full access to it just by being there. Then imagine that your children are born with a starry sky with unending twinkling stars within them that make up their entire selves. They radiate and feel loved and are seen in their complete harmony, which belongs to the privilege of the newborn.

As your children grow older, this extraordinary and unique view of them starts to change. Your attitudes shift from 'you are perfect as you are' to 'I need you to behave in a specific way'. They are no longer unique as they are (well, in your mind maybe, but not in your actions) and they must now learn to adapt to what you find acceptable in daily life. Your own shadows are brought to life and can no longer be kept down. Things about the way your child behaves awaken something in you that you hadn't expected, and you start to counter them with the same reactions that helped you survive. Naturally, everyone in a civilised world needs to adapt to the norms and rules of the culture in which they live. What was previously praised in your child's behaviour and found unique and perfect is no longer so. You begin to extinguish star after star in their sky without realising it. Suddenly, it is inappropriate to burp after dinner. It used to be funny and a sign of positive energy when your child banged the spoon on the table. Now it is disturbing and wrong. Phrases like 'don't do it', 'such behaviour is not acceptable', 'stop when I say so', 'do this, do that' become commonplace, and your child is not lauded and recognised as earlier.

The thing is that your child relies on you and will trust what you teach them. When one depends on your parents for survival, you suppress the parts that they disapprove of and exaggerate the approved parts. Perhaps you express enthusiasm as you have seen your mother do, or outbursts of anger like your father. Grief is subdued because it is not acknowledged, and you keep fear to yourself because you don't want to worry your parents. You learn that to be accepted, you will need to adjust yourself to fit into the culturally approved norms, accepted by your close family or caregivers and those you associate with. Only specific parts of your character are accepted and approved and see the light of day. Other parts will be hidden in the unknown places of your being, hidden in the shadows, which means that some of your lit-up stars are switched off as they seem to lose their functionality, or at least that is how your adjusted self begins to differentiate the world of yours, putting it into categories of what are appreciated and acceptable behaviours and what are not. This shift is barely visible, and it is quite difficult to pin down how this process evolves, as it is very slow. But by repeating the same sequences over and over again, you slowly teach your children that only certain behaviours are acceptable and lovable.

I once had a teenager in therapy who had a hard time feeling his inner emotional life, and therefore could not express how he felt if he was upset, mad, or scared. Because of this, he was struggling with his ability to show love. He was very afraid to open up, but also he did not have the words to identify his feelings. Therefore, a significant part of him was never unfolded, which made life difficult for him. As a child, he often became quite emotional and cried or had outbursts of anger, to which he was repeatedly told by his father: 'Stop being a pussy, be a man!' He was brought up believing that crying was a bad thing and that emotions were inappropriate. That is how he learnt to hide his own emotions. As a result of this, several stars on his starry sky went out one after the other – being emotional and expressive were not valued, and slowly the boy adjusted accordingly to the set of values that were, and drove this gentle and sensitive side of himself into the shadows while learning to behave 'dispassionately'. When he reached puberty, he unconsciously began to deal with the two parts of himself, one that he wanted to suppress, and one to which he was trying to give life. It was his survival strategy that lodged in his subconscious, with everything he unknowingly had begun to reject of himself – the unacceptable and unwanted parts – which got the tender, sensitive star extinguished. He was slowly beginning to drown in loneliness. By shedding light on the unconscious strategies he had learnt, he could begin to support the parts that he had unintentionally suppressed and begin to turn on the light in his formative time. This awareness created the greatest change in him. Being able to register and acknowledge his inner emotional life helped him express his feelings and not let himself be controlled by the shadows of his parents. That way, he slowly learnt to set boundaries and listen to himself and be true to what felt best for him. He still struggles, returning to his old pattern when with his father. Still, the awareness of what is happening in himself and the understanding that he is meeting one of his father's shadows makes it more bearable for him.

This is what happens all the time when old, ingrained patterns are repeated without you even noticing it. My intention is not to make you feel guilty or afraid of damaging your teen. These are pretty common survival strategies that everyone employs to a greater or lesser extent. But it's possible that you suspect that you are hurting your teenager or turning off too many stars. In that case, this is just an example to help you understand what it looks like and how it works.

A life's work

My childhood was in many ways amazing, safe and extremely privileged. Yet, I did get some wounds that haunted me during my adolescence and early adulthood. My parents divorced when I was three years old, so I don't have that many memories of them together. I grew up with my mother and had frequent, close and wonderful contact with my father. My mother is an amazing woman, smart and analytical, with a beautiful and fine heart. Yet she also carried her personal struggles from pain in her life – let's call them her shadows or her extinguished stars. She was definitely at her best in the very difficult and harder conversations. She felt safe and at home and could keep analysing for hours. Only there did she feel the value of the conversation. When I disappointed her or provoked something in her unconsciously, she used her eyes to express her dissatisfaction by looking through me, as if I was not in the room. Sometimes, she could be icy cold and distant, and I always cried inside when that happened. At the same time, I made sure to be sweet and do good things for her. I helped with cleaning, cooking, and gave her extraordinary gifts while 'pleasing' her. All this I did unconsciously so as not to be penalised with her coldness, and in the hope that she would see me and notice everything I did for her – so that, hopefully, one day, she would tell me that she loved me.

I was a bright and cheerful child and would come home happy from kindergarten or school and tell her about something fun or wonderful that had happened. She would start pondering and ask a lot of interrogating questions about my experiences so that I often would end up tearful. Unconsciously, I represented the stars in her that had been extinguished or overshadowed many years earlier. My easy and positive way of being in the world triggered her extinguished stars from when she was a child. Although she came from an affluent, academic family, she lost a beloved little sister who died of cancer as a child. A year after this, her new-born little brother died too. So it is clear that her childhood was heavy and sad with parents who themselves struggled to survive and therefore were unable to be caring and present in my mother's life. For that reason, with her sharp gaze she found the bad in the good, designated the darkness that she knew the best and I learnt that we could find closeness and cohesion in this way. I felt loved when she prioritised this time with me. In reality, I was defenceless and sensitive of her rejection, and I did not feel worthy of receiving her love. Part of my young psyche would work hard trying to hide the pain of rejection far away from my conscious self, and my survival strategies replaced it with a much better defence mechanism that worked well for me. I became her interlocutor in pain and extinguished a star inside myself, to feel a connection with my mother. To get what I longed for, closeness and connection.

My mother is still alive, and I love her dearly. Our pattern – which was not about accommodating my joy and letting my traits grow and flourish – came to influence our relationship for many years. I needed her attention, support and acknowledgement even when I knew it would make me sad and unfulfilled, so I learnt to switch off and adapt to the norms of her own unknowingly extinguished stars. But on an unconscious level, there was still a part of me which instinctively knew that this was not how things should be, nor how a child should feel. Something within me knew it shouldn't be like that – and that I deserved to feel better about myself and who I was – so I rebelled in a childish and unconstructive manner as I became a teenager. Every time I spoke up and began to oppose and question her strategies, I was informed that I was too demanding or simply too much. I am confident my mother had no intention of letting me feel this way. It was all taking place unconsciously because of her hidden stars. She did what she did because she was taught in her own youth that this would be a beneficial survival strategy for her, maybe even a way to feel connected to her own parents. I mostly recall how unfair this felt to me. Later on, I learnt how to cultivate the ability to not become overly excited or overly sad, frustrated, or happy. I stayed right in the middle to avoid rocking my mum's boat, to avoid any unpleasantness. Yet the important part here is that just because I no longer allowed that part of myself to shine did not mean that it would have disappeared from my mental structure. It helped me avoid getting hurt, which felt safe and secure for my survival strategies. An essential part of me got cut off in my safe environment. But the consequence of that was that it became impossible for me to fully express myself authentically and to feel whole.

In evolutionary terms, suppressing some parts of ourselves has been about survival. It is a necessary survival strategy that belongs to all of us. Look at me; I sensed a better connection with my mother if we could talk about pain or sadness. I listened dutifully as the dangers of the world were brought up, and I was able to imagine what was waiting to unfold. In these intense conversations, we became deeply connected, and I felt loved and seen. That's because we shared something that made her feel safe and secure. I was aware that it didn't feel right for me, but I did not understand the actual dynamics surrounding it as a child. So, of course I continued to do what made me feel seen by her, which gave me a feeling of significance. I learnt to listen and analyse and be in the more complex areas of life. And the consequence of that was that it was necessary to put a lid on the positive parts of me that were now bound up within me. A side of me that I dreamt would be accepted and appreciated by her every second of every day, yet I did not have the language to express my longing at that time.

The unconscious assumption in the story about my mother and me was that I felt my joy and light-hearted energy were not lovable. I had to turn off these particular stars within me to make her feel safe and in control. Of course, it was not intentional on her part. She did the best she could with the resources available from what she had learnt, but the pain of life she carried around inside resulted in her unknowingly passing her extinguished stars on to me. I had to learn to find a way to deal with the unconscious contract we had made. Of course, I did not want to become her confidante and co-carrier of her life pain. First, I needed to become aware of the pattern; I had to put some light on it by learning to put less pressure on myself and, eventually, to allow myself to light up my own stars again and fully embrace the person I am.

Our shadow is made up of all the parts of ourselves that we hide, deny, suppress, and don't see in ourselves – both the positive and the negative. Our shadow is all the aspects that we reject out of shame, fear or disapproval. It is made up of any part of ourselves that we believe is unacceptable, will be met with disapproval by others, or that annoys, horrifies or disgusts us about other people or about ourselves.

Debbie Ford, co-author of *The Shadow Effect*

Domino pieces

You will unconsciously pass your extinguished stars on to your children, if you are not cognisant of them. 'You name it, you tame it,' as Daniel Siegel puts it. Simply being aware of and paying attention to your extinguished stars will help you to minimise and change their negative influence. In some sense, you must name the shadow. These ideas were first introduced in the West by psychologist Carl Jung. He described the shadow as 'the unconscious and disowned parts of your personality that the ego fails to see, acknowledge, and accept'. It is an aspect of yourselves that is not exposed to the light of your consciousness. Debbie Ford delved into the dark sides of life and how to face the shadows. She was the author and personal transformation coach who brought Jung's work into modern times.

Your wounds will become your children's wounds over time. Your pain will be passed on unless you work on bringing light to your shadow sides and help yourself resolve them. You will simply copy-and-paste the same patterns that your parents gave you onto your children, unless you purposefully try to identify which shadows or, as I call them, extinguished stars do not belong to you, and let your stars light up again. That way, you are better able to ensure your children's stars can shine. Not that you will ever succeed 100 per cent, but a step in the right direction is better than no steps at all. When you deny an aspect of yourself it doesn't disappear. It just fades away from your conscious awareness, and this knowledge is a good reminder to keep on working on yourself when it feels meaningless.

The challenge is that many find it difficult and uncomfortable to begin identifying their abandoned or extinguished stars. It is a sensitive area, perhaps shameful, and can feel daunting to approach. Many do not begin this journey because a new awareness requires new behaviour and habits. This in turn requires energy and dedication and it often can feel easier to do nothing. One should approach the challenge with the same pragmatism, courage and curiosity needed to understand and solve any other task in life. I wish it would become as commonplace as solving any maths problem, for example.

If I had not listened to my gut feeling and patiently worked on ways to change the unconscious behaviour that I knew I had – especially changing my tendency to use my gaze to control my surroundings – I would have passed this unhealthy trait on to my children like domino pieces. I would have sent the same subtle messages to them as I had received. But then the cardinal point of our relationship would have been focused on me and not on them and their needs. This is the bare and harsh truth that I have come to realise. I share this with you because I believe there is a need for more openness in a world of tamed emotions and unmet needs. Most people do not understand what creates turmoil within them and therefore do not have the awareness or tools to handle the problem. The outcome can put a barrier between your children and you.

You must take your subconscious emotions into your own hands and look at them with a lot more love and understanding; reframe your focus. Reframing is the only tool which will enable you to heal and change conditions for the better. If not, you will continue to navigate from your old, ingrained patterns, which will put burdens on your teenager to deal with later on in life. They will recognise that something seems unfair but will adjust their outlook and behaviour accordingly as long as they are still dependent on you. There is a reason why children of alcoholics become alcoholics themselves, or why a child who has been assaulted physically or mentally becomes violent. Always strive to understand their need to feel loved, to be seen and valued. Children are adaptable and super quick to spot how to behave to receive love and attention; even if their needs are not fully met, they will find a way.

Make the unconscious conscious

Many of you are probably most comfortable dealing with your own happy emotions and less so with your troublesome ones. You want your self-image to be positive, because facing all our shortcomings requires each and all of us to enter the door to shame and despair. Who wants that? Not many, I am sure, but the outcome is a strong investment in how you will be able to relate and be there for your children, as well as

investing in helping them relate and deal with their own personal challenges down the generations. Danes do not believe
in an always happy ending, without worries, challenges and
self-examination. But, rather, in the truthful, honest life that
embraces everyday experiences for better or worse, focusing
on growth and on the ability to look for the positive.

If you are not genuine and don't let yourself express who
you really are, you will never be capable of creating the life
that you dream of. You can't make a life that's truthful to
you if you're not capable of being true to yourself and the
people surrounding you. Without inner work, it is not possible
to become a good role model and to teach your teenager to
create the life they dream of. I tell my daughters about the
things from my childhood that have hurt me. I share my life
for better or worse, focusing on the wisdom it has given me.
Without these experiences, I would not be the person I am
today and would not have had the opportunity to break the
circle of extinguished stars, or at least to lessen their influence.
I let my daughters know they can always come to me and tell
me if I hurt them or push their limits too much. I will always
listen to them, take their words seriously, and do my best to
be the only carrier of my own pain. That's a key thing, and
it makes conscious parenting very authentic. Furthermore,
when you do the work of reframing your own wounds you will
also allow yourself to shine fully. So, it is actually a win–win
situation.

If my mother had been aware of her extinguished stars –
her shadows – she would have been able to let my stars unfold
fully and shine instead of turning them off by making me

feel like I was wrong and too demanding. But to do that, she would have needed to be authentically present and connect from an open heart. For that, she would have had to fully connect with herself, which means she would have had to do her necessary work to understand her own shadows, and thereby her projections, fully. In that lies the essence of conscious parenting; you can only succeed in changing your unconscious parenting patterns if you are willing to grasp the root of which hurt feelings or unmet needs you carry around. One is dependent on the other.

Learning to be a conscious parent is not about becoming a perfect parent but, rather, about being authentic and asking yourself: *What is controlling my behaviour right now? Am I acting unconsciously or consciously? How can I take 'time out' to calm down before returning to my teenager? How can I learn to embrace every little twinkling star within me to help it illuminate fully?* Questions like these are essential in the process of practising being a conscious parent. Then you'll be able to do something different to what your parents did. The goal is never perfection; the goal is investment and willingness to break a pattern, especially when the emotional brain has a grip on you.

None of us is actually in balance 100 per cent of the time and acting rationally, focusing on strengthening the stars already shining within our teens. What you can do is learn to become aware of the ways that you are reacting unconsciously. Then you'll be better able to think before you respond to stimuli, 'I feel triggered because something that comes from a place within, where I was not loved or challenged as a child, is provoked.'

The strategy I learnt was to fight for my survival. I don't need to do that any longer, because I embrace the young me, comfort her and let her know that she doesn't have to feel hurt any more. She *is* loved. Therefore, when my teenagers trigger me, I can respond from a place that allows the stars in them to shine, and I can feel at peace within. When you are aware and present, you can take a step back; you can even leave the room to avoid responding unconsciously and take some breaths to restore your inner balance. I do not believe that I will ever succeed completely, turning on my own extinguished stars and being fully healed. Therefore, I will probably end up endlessly extinguishing stars in my daughters. I think that is something I will have to come to terms with. But I will attempt to always do my best, and I do not demand more of myself than that.

Being a conscious parent is a choice and can be a healthy path for you personally and for your way of being a parent. Projection and triggers are red flags that must be investigated. Children trigger, but so do adolescents. Young children are still in your control while slowly slipping out of your hands when they become teenagers. To always work on the relationship and continue building on a close contact, time with teenagers mustn't be filled with conflicts. You must therefore rediscover the extinguished stars in yourself and work on polishing them again and again until they begin to sparkle. The starry sky only forms your whole self when it includes both the extinguished and the shining stars. Hence, find the cause of the turmoil within that many of us sense but do not quite understand. Only certain parts of you are recognised and fulfilled, but the extinguished stars in your starry sky are still part of who you are, no matter how hidden they are. They do not disappear; they are just not lit up any more. It is the starry sky in its entirety that makes us unique, not just half of it.

The gift

You would not know as you enter parenthood that your children will become your most important teachers. They will mirror and reflect your entire self, your shadows, extinguished stars and broken emotions back at you because they are still so completely open and unspoiled. Conscious parenting is all about changing the focus from how your teenagers should be handled to how you should handle yourself. Which means becoming more aware of the baggage you bring with you in an effort to ensure your children and teens grow up with greater love for themselves and for the world they live in.

Today, as a mother, I know that my teens have needs, and that I have needs, which are not necessarily the same. I must figure out which needs should be listened to first. I can then turn to my daughters aware that I have worked on how to balance my starting point. I make an effort to understand the parts of me that I had to close down because they were not valued or recognised the way that they were meant to be. These parts weren't appreciated and therefore they were suppressed until I learnt how to give them first aid so they could come back to life and be healed properly. I have consciously changed some things which I feared might stand in the way of my girls' ability to unfold their full potential. I want them to grow up with the knowledge that they are unconditionally loved for who they are and not for what they do. Sometimes I still struggle to allow myself and my girls to feel complete joy. A trace of scepticism still lives within me since I learnt at a young age that there is always something bad in the good. Although I know today, intellectually, that this does not have to be the truth, it is perhaps the biggest barrier that I still face every day. I tell myself that it is not my fault. I am candid with my girls when I fail to live up to my own aspirations. Self-awareness and self-healing are lifelong processes, a work that will never end. That is something I still work on accepting. Despite my shortcomings, my daughters are loved thoroughly and exactly as they are. I will do everything I can to make sure they continue to feel loved.

I believe that close and meaningful contact with your teenager is the most important gift that you can give them in their way through life. That means that they will have a good foundation which can bring them greater satisfaction in life. Begin with yourselves. Become aware of what your own sky looks like. Let your starry sky light up and pass its beauty on to your teenagers, rather than the dark and half-covered sky. Deep down, this is what we all want to pass on to our children, to give them unconditional love and send them out into the world in the best way possible so that they can have a good life unburdened by the legacy of previous generations. They deserve to be themselves, whole and beloved as they are.

CHAPTER 3

Trust

RULE NUMBER ONE

Why is Denmark still ranked high when it comes to being one of the happiest countries in the world? One answer is found in the six areas described in *The Danish Way of Parenting*, and another is *trust*, also called 'social capital'. Trust is an expression of a sense of community that transcends the boundaries of our society, which is expressed in the old phrase, 'A man's word is his bond.'

Trust is an emotion and is the phenomenon that is manifested by an individual having an expectation or belief that another individual is trustworthy. In Greek and Old Norse, (to) trust is the same as (to have) faith. According to K. E. Løgstrup, Danish philosopher and theologian, people's trust is innate, whereas mistrust is learnt while growing up.

When I was a child, our front door was never locked, and neighbours, friends and family came visiting when they walked by. There was always a welcoming and open atmosphere, and I felt safe and good. Many years later, when I moved into a house with my husband, we did not lock our door, to begin with, either – only at night. I wanted to bring the same state of trusting energy into my life with children, as I liked it so much when I grew up. It only lasted a short time, as I had to adopt fear of intruders into my life when someone I knew had an experience of a burglar who broke into their home at night when they were all asleep. As my children walked home from school by themselves, I couldn't risk them bumping into anyone who wasn't welcome. Their safety was my first priority, of course, and we started to lock our doors. No wonder Danes are said to be one of the most trusting people on earth!

The essence of trust

Danish society is a place of trust; it is a concept that we value highly and can be seen rooted in long periods of stability and transparency in our democracy and low degree of corruption. Some also believe that the value of social networking is a crucial player, part of the formation that we bring into everything we do – a circle from adult to child, who grows up with ingrained norms and repeats this joyous and rewarding cycle that gives us strong confidence in each other. A high level of trust has great value for a nation: socially, politically, and economically. It creates a public culture characterised by reciprocity and co-operation, and commitment to common laws and agreements. Trust helps create well-being, security and credible relationships between people, and makes community life function more easily. The former Danish prime minister Poul Nyrup Rasmussen once stated that 'You rarely see a Dane with a knife in his hand without a fork in the other.' Drive along the small, idyllic, country roads in the summer. You will find small unguarded stalls with freshly picked strawberries, peas, newly dug potatoes, carrots, honey, flowers, etc., for sale. There is only a small cash box where the money is put, so only a matter of trust makes such a purchase possible. Suppose you ask a Dane for directions. In that case, you can be sure that you will not be shown to a blind alley, and even though we may seem a little private, we will in general always meet strangers with trust.

It is also well known that we Danes like to let our babies sleep in their strollers outside cafes or restaurants, while we enjoy a little socialising with friends – even when it is freezing cold. This is a quite common practice, although, of course, there is always an open line via the baby monitor if the child wakes up. Some readers may remember what happened to a Danish mother who, in 1997, let her 14-month-old daughter sleep in the pram outside a cafe in New York. She could see the stroller through the window and did not think this could create any concerns. The police were called, and she was arrested. She was later released when she explained that this is what we do in Denmark. Trying to steal a pram off the street has only been tried a few times here, but fortunately without much success.

Of course, Denmark is a relatively safe country. Most teens do not struggle daily with gang conflicts, crime, poverty, or drugs. It is reasonably safe to roam the streets day and night, and no one has to worry about their children being kidnapped or shot. Unfortunately, this is not the reality in other countries. I can only imagine how frightening it must be. Denmark is not perfect. Here, too, loneliness, anxiety and other challenges are present, and there is room for improvement, for sure. However, overall, it is safe and secure to live here, making it a lot easier to trust other people and to be trustworthy.

I like to believe that our ongoing ability to show that we are trustworthy towards each other – strangers, acquaintances and close relations – is a true characteristic of who we are. For me, trust is to let go of fear. It may be that I imagine my daughters getting hurt or, worse, sick, or that I experience someone who does not wish me well. If I want to get out of my negative thoughts, I tell myself that it is going to be OK. Everything will work out fine, and I put a lid on my fear so that I can trust in some kind of a bigger meaning of what unfolds. Trust for me is also about having an expectation that a given norm is respected, and daring to believe that others will not cheat and inflict a loss on me. As Lao Tzu stated: 'He who does not trust enough, will not be trusted.'

A conscious choice

We often take what seems natural and obvious to us for granted, even though the same norms and expectations do not necessarily exist for others. That is what makes life beautiful in its sometimes-brutal diversity. I may be naive, but when I interact with other people, I go into it with full confidence in them. Since I want to be enriched by the energy and competencies of others, and to give of everything I have, unconditional trust is an absolutely crucial prerequisite for me. I do not know how human relations can be done differently. After all, I would never collaborate or interact with someone if I did not believe that I could trust them. I think everyone deserves a chance, and I appreciate being met with the same openness. Of course, if someone steps on my toes, I will withdraw after giving them the benefit of a doubt or two. And that sometimes happens. Nevertheless, I sincerely believe that meeting others with an open heart is the best way to be in the world, making it a better place. Therefore, I would also describe my conscious naivety as my strength of hope.

It goes without saying that besides the fact that the building blocks in Danish society are made on trust, trust is of great importance in our educational system as well, where social training is just as important as mathematics and language. Students learn early that better results are achieved by working in teams and co-operating on tasks. That the community built around togetherness and collaboration strengthens trust and empathy and fosters a good learning environment. That success is based on collaboration, and collaboration cannot work optimally if there is no trust. Being around classmates in good faith and with people who wish to make you a better person in a collective progressive relationship positively shapes your view of the world. You learn that life is a 'safe' place and that people generally want the best for you. And, when you are treated in this way by others, it awakens the same in you, and the bond of trust is established.

Knowing that trust is not in doubt is also an integral part of the set of norms that unfolds in most families. Obviously, I paint with broad brushstrokes, as there are plenty of examples of the opposite. However, the construction bricks of trust are also brought into the way we do family life here.

In the relationship I have with my daughters, trust is a crucial component. I see it as the glue between us that makes us close in a shared, deep commitment. If I can count on my girls, they get the freedom they want. That is because trust has always been the marker that has meant everything in whatever we have done together. They respect the agreements we make jointly, and they know that we trust them unconditionally. It is vital for our family dynamics that this works optimally, and it is therefore a conscious choice. It provides security and a more robust family structure; having such a foundation to stand on is crucial for those times containing problems and challenges. And we have had our hurdles to deal with, from the top of the mountains to the lowest of the valleys.

The thing is that trust isn't something that comes out of the blue; it is something that must be practised, and (even better) from the early years of parenthood. This is not to say that it is too late when the teenage years have knocked on your little pumpkin's door – it is never too late. Wherever you are on that line, you will experience a safe place built when consciously giving trust and therefore receiving even more. What your teen and you will share with each other – or spouse, friend, or colleague – is the building block for a happier and more worry-free life. Sure, there will be plenty of episodes where you can't live up to such a high standard, which is human and OK – the same goes for your children – but you move on and make sure to articulate what happened and take ownership of not living up to your best intentions. That fosters trust.

What often happens, though, when your cute and lovable children become teenagers, is that you change your expectations and react more harshly if they do not live up to the trust you give them. Trust until adolescence has been carried by reciprocity. It now becomes a more one-way demand from you to them. Your understanding and forbearance suddenly disappear and are replaced by a greater degree of distrust, looking for instances of your teens not taking responsibility well enough – a distrust, which you assume in advance, that has the opposite effect from what you want.

Interacting with your teenagers and fulfilling your adult, leadership role is all about communicating your values through your behaviour. It is about dialogue and engagement. Knowing your values will make it easier to set limits and to talk about what you like and don't like as individuals and as a family (much more about this can be found in my online course). Reframe your language instead of using ultimatums.

Walking over the bridge

Your teen needs you to trust in them, and that is the key essence you must remind yourself of daily if you feel the temptation to freak out. It is worth it. A way to do this is to try to understand your teenager's point of view and learn about their wishes and desires while not controlling and directing their lives too much. It can be difficult sometimes and, especially in this fast-paced world, you are going to overrule them when they try to say some things to you: 'Mum, all the others are going to a party on Friday, can I go?' 'No, honey, I don't think you are ready to party yet.' Or: 'Daddy, is it normal to feel nervous when someone is approaching me?' 'Son, if you are a real man, you show confidence and keep your head upright.'

In both these cases, you are more conscious of your own perspectives and needs than being aware of what is going on in your teen's inner world. Because of that, you won't come across as someone striving to do your best to nurture their trust in you. Instead, you show them that they are not worth listening to. But they are, so you must tell yourself that your behaviour is a reminder that you are too distant and stressed and will benefit from some time to connect with your teen. In that case, it works so that if your teen shows by their actions that you can trust them, they are given the freedom to do what they want within a reasonable framework.

When you listen actively with your full attention, you walk over the bridge to where your teen is – metaphorically – that is very respectfully. You listen, wanting to understand how it is to be on this side of the bridge. Your teen will most likely be standing in another way than you prefer and might not see the full view of the surroundings as you do. Your teen could be more concerned about whether any of their friends see that their parents exist, or just happy you came the long way over to their still smaller world.

Try it out. I use sentences such as: 'I hear you.' 'I'm here for you, and I won't leave you.' 'It sounds amazing.' 'Did you really say that?' 'How were you able to do this?' 'A party on Friday, that sounds fun. Tell me a little more about it.' 'Thank you for sharing all this with me. It really warms my heart, and of course, it is normal to feel nervous sometimes.' 'You will be good.' When you have listened to your teen and really put yourselves in their shoes, you empathise with what you have heard and walk back to the side of the bridge where you, as the parent, belong. Those two places are not the same.

The more you give room to really listen, the more you learn about yourself and others, resulting in more understanding, inclusiveness and trust. This applies not only in stressful situations but in every type of social interaction. By being a good listening role model for your teen, you give them one of the greatest gifts in life. When you genuinely listen to what others have to say, rather than just waiting for your chance to speak, you teach them the importance of listening patiently and enquiring with an open and curious mind. Therein lies the art of talking together, so you understand and trust each other better.

The act of speaking itself has little value. Being able to connect with other people through conversation has. Trust is the building block that needs to be present and valued. It is clear, in every aspect, when trust is present, for it is then that your teen dares to confide in you, itself an essential source of well-being and belonging. Where else is it OK to fail except at home in a safe harbour, to be inadequate, unreasonable, and too much? It is the greatest gift you can give your children – that they are allowed to be unreasonable and imperfect in a safe environment and with the certainty that even if they behave unlovingly, they are loved anyway, unconditionally.

There is no trust if there is an unequal relationship between your teenager and you. There is an implicit assumption of mistrust when you don't talk with but only at your teen: 'Do the dishes.' 'Don't make a big deal out of it.' Talking at is when you speak to someone not expecting a back-and-forth dialogue with mutual input, like a waterfall rushing down endlessly without anything stopping it. The stream only goes one way. There is always the risk of being tricked implicit with mistrust. Imagine the history, knowledge and all the stars that have been extinguished for those who resort to this strategy. Most often, it is used by someone who has experienced being talked to like that and who has learnt that this is the way it works best. Maybe it works for some people, but this is not the case for me. Such a way of communicating is precisely what undermines the trust that I am aiming for and asking my teens to comply with. I hope it is possible to spot the contrast and see why talking at is so one-dimensional: you cannot both trust and not trust your teen. When that happens, it is because you have been caught by fear, old stories, thoughts, shadows, etc., yourself.

You must remember that you are the creators of the best circumstances for everyone in the family to thrive and feel loved. Sometimes I think we hastily relinquish the guiding and framing role that our teenagers still need. Because they are autonomous in many things does not mean that we must release the clutch and drive in neutral. No, it is now that everything we have built on while they were little is being practised. It is now that the trust between us must deepen and become even stronger. You show that you are worth trusting, and, at the same time, your teen must show that they are trustworthy too. The synergy is a two-way consensus. This is where the springboard is. Perhaps you need to find the answer to why Danish teenagers come out of their youth roughly unscathed, even though they carry all aspects of being a teenager with them as everyone else.

You are what you remember

It is no secret that teenagers sometimes behave unstably or react with aloofness and indifference for no apparent reason. Again, you must keep in mind that the transition from child to adult is happening, where they try and test what they like and do not like. They don't know it yet and will have to explore the nooks and crannies of life to get to know themselves. They need the experience to form their selves and their starry sky.

The moment you begin to trust less that your teen is trustworthy, then a vicious circle of unfulfilled agreements and frequent quarrels can start, which in turn will weaken the trust between you more and lead to further breaches of trust. No one can ever always be the perfect guiding light unless you see flaws and mistakes as the ideal way to show your children what humanity looks like. Trust has its roots in being honest and sincere, and not shying away from your own flaws.

Most of the boys and girls that I know in my professional

work and through my children have grown up with this kind of agreement between them and their parents. Here is my experience: if you show your teen that you believe in them early, they live up to it. If you just fleetingly suggest that you don't, you have sowed seeds of division. It is that simple; if the times when trust has been intact are all-dominating, this will be the case. A colleague once asked how, when I was a teacher, I always managed to get the big boys in the graduating classes to take out the trash from the class after school. I replied that I always told them I knew they would do it. They knew I was counting on them, whereas with the other teachers, they were met with distrust that they would remember to do it. Therefore, they lived up to the fact that there was no expectation that they would do it. So why make an effort?

There is a psychological phenomenon that describes how expectations can modify behaviour. It is called the Pygmalion effect and it provides evidence for self-fulfilling prophecy, which is based on the idea that others' beliefs about you become true because their belief impacts how you behave.

Robert Rosenthal is a German-born American psychologist and professor. He is best known for the Pygmalion effect, aka the Rosenthal effect, which refers to the psychological phenomenon that the greater the beliefs and expectations on individuals, often children and students, the better they function. The Pygmalion effect is self-amplifying in both negative and positive directions.

What can you do if you live in a country that is not based on trust in the same way as Denmark, and you want to develop more trust in your teenager? Do not worry. Trust comes from within and can be built and cherished everywhere. You set the standard in the family yourself, and it will spread to others around you. You live up to what is expected of you, no matter where you come from.

When Danish teenagers start going to parties and drinking some alcohol, a framework is set for how many drinks may be drunk and what time to come home in agreement with the teenager. So it was in our family. It may be that one or two beers are OK with a return home by 10 p.m. If the plans change with regards to the location or otherwise, the teenager must always notify their parents either by calling or texting. If this works flawlessly over a reasonable period, the agreement can be extended according to need and situation, but always with a mutually valid trust. I always tell my teens that I trust and have full confidence in them. Which I have. We do not differ from many other Danes in my family, and it works very well for most. This kind of agreement gives peace of mind to both the parents and the teen. As a bonus, you avoid your teenager needing to break all boundaries and challenge the rules that have been set in the negotiation because they have been made in a shared understanding.

I would like to point out that being a parent who prefers to communicate equally with your teenagers, listening, and agreeing on some decisions, is *not* the same as being permissive, weak, or twisted around their little finger. It is imperative to set a clear framework and say 'no' sometimes. And stick to the no if necessary. Do not let these two things be mixed. To be a transparent, stable and trustworthy parent, you must stand firm on the norms and values that form the framework of a safe childhood in a home with respect and love and many stars sparkling. Not rigid, but with an underlying foundation that you build on healthily. In order to function with an equal and meaningful trust between you and your teenagers, you must be able to listen, understand and be prepared to meet their needs when it comes to chores and decisions that belong to everyday life. If there is no trust, there is no co-operation on anything else.

CHAPTER 4

Play

BUILDING INDEPENDENCE AND CHARACTER

Adolescence is when everything we have taught our children so far, both the conscious and the unconscious aspects, will be tested and practised. This is a necessary part of our teens' development, to feel in their own body where they can relate or not. They need to make what they have learnt feel meaningful to them and actively decide to bring it further into their life. It is a healthy and natural process if we have raised our children to make independent, sustainable decisions and choices in life with as large and sparkling starry sky as possible. This process will happen, and therefore a new view of free play is recommended.

Play teaches self-control, inner drive, stress control, negotiation and co-operation. It encourages creativity, imagination and empathy, which increases well-being.

Redefining play

As parents, we often fall into the hole of having predetermined opinions about what our teen should do and how we want them to behave responsibly and maturely. We want them to remain spontaneous and playful in life, but we have not yet figured out what playfulness looks like when they are no longer children. Is play now adult-led activities, gambling, partying with friends, drinking alcohol, or being an influencer on social media? What does 'free play' look like in adolescence, when teens are no longer jumping in puddles, climbing trees, or immersing themselves in buglife? We dream that they will interact across age, gender, ethnicity and language barriers simply because play is universal and works best when unstructured and still educational. However, it seems unclear what to expect from this age. It is easy to state that teens can simply play in nature – or play board games, which many adolescents do in Denmark. They are very fond of this *hygge* time with their friends, where they are challenged intellectually while still being around like-minded people. Still, once we have seen the natural developmental phase that comes with age, it is clear that interests are changing. Hence the importance of play.

The characteristics of free, unstructured play are the cardinal point. Through the universe of free play, the child learns to solve problems, relate to other people, and what boundaries are, and they become clearer about what feels good or bad. These are the same characteristics that are cultivated in adolescence, and which need to come alive in a completely new setting. This understanding of your teenager suddenly gives a whole new picture of what is at stake. Those who have followed me and my work over the years and know what I stand for are therefore aware that I am a great champion of free play and its significance for self-direction and resilience. In coming to understand how teenagers play, I have concluded that Russian psychologist Lev Vygotsky's ideas about the zone of proximal development still apply. With teens, play is no longer free play as we know it – it is now expressed as liberation, critical thinking, spontaneity, and the formation of 'my independent self'. Some like to call it formation, others prefer character building. As author Elmer G. Letterman states: 'It takes personality to open doors, but it takes character to keep them open.'

Lev Vygotsky (1896–1934) was a Soviet psychologist known for his work on psychological development in children, and best known for his concept of the zone of proximal development (ZPD). The zone of proximal development is defined by 'the distance between the actual developmental level as determined by independent problem solving and the level of potential development as determined through problem solving under adult guidance or in collaboration with more capable peers.'

Free play is the metaphor for the independence phase. Your teenager will, with your support, take small new steps towards becoming whole individuals who can find peace in themselves with as many lit stars in the sky as possible. The building blocks to this come in many forms and with many nuances. Despite the advent of new definitions of free play, for me there must always be a degree of rest for the brain; an opportunity not to have to process information and impressions but instead to let go and recharge.

Duties

Don't choke on your coffee! It may not feel like play for most teens to participate in household chores, not even for you, but that is how I like to express it.

If you start early on, before adolescence, with your children participating in household chores in a way that makes it fun and a way to be together, it will feel quite natural for them to carry on doing such chores when they reach adolescence. Maybe they will try to wriggle out of it, feel unmotivated or busy, but I have come across the least motivation to avoid their responsibilities when they experience the benefits of being able to 'zone out'. I have seen my daughters tilt into another state and let their thoughts and inner moods calm down when they vacuum or walk our dog – giving them confidence in their own abilities while handling their thoughts.

Household duties provide a break while your teen nurtures new skills. With music on in the background (which appeals to many teens), it gives a necessary break from everyday pressures and expectations, informal and non-controlling. Such a break is healthy and essential, and with a confirmed agreement created in collaboration with the teenager about expectations, frameworks and tasks, this free space also provides an opportunity to grow mentally and feel meaningful. In the spirit of Vygotsky, your teen acquires and refines knowledge that is in their proximal developmental zone. It is the implicit gift in the redefined play for teens.

In my family, my daughters have always been involved in cooking. When they were little, they sat at the kitchen table, helping to peel potatoes, or cut cucumbers into cubes, knead dough, or shape meatballs. When they were about 10 or 11 years old, they got a fixed day during the week when they were in charge of dinner. They have always had to clean their own room, clear the table after we've eaten, help load the dishwasher, and go for a walk with the dog when needed. Together we have made it work. We depend on each other and each other's contribution to the family. Of course, my husband and I carry the responsibility – and nothing is forced – but it is a value we decide to live out. My kids have been given pocket money, but not because they help at home. This is not something for which they should be paid. It is part of being in a family and, therefore, something natural to commit to. I know many do it differently. My daughters get pocket money because they must learn to manage finances sensibly and take responsibility for it, figuring out how to save money if they desperately want something. I think the understanding lies in discovering that things cost, and that money must therefore be managed with consideration to not disappear.

When teenagers are given household duties as an area of responsibility, you show them trust and equality. You let them know that you believe in them and their abilities. For many years, my oldest daughter Ida experimented with making cakes based on her imagination and the glimpses she had when she helped me with baking. She had only captured fractions of what a good cake should contain, but she was given free rein to try it out, and out of the oven came cakes in all sorts of colours and shapes. They usually tasted like gum and were inedible. Still, she got credit for her interest and curiosity in learning to bake without help, and, of course, I always ate a little to satisfy her. The older she got, the more she understood what was needed, and today is good at baking cakes and is an excellent chef. Learning by doing really works.

Taking a role in the household chores is part of the formation process that is good for your teenager. Only very few people experience a life where others take care of them, where they do not have to contribute to the community. The rest of us must learn to make everyday life work with duties, which also applies to our teens. You are preparing them for the future by simply not correcting or commenting on the outcome. Let them be and do it their way – acknowledge the process and their attempt to do it as best they can, not the result. It builds self-esteem and the belief that their contribution means something in the big picture. Children and teens grow from having responsibilities that they can fulfil. From being challenged just enough for them to master it. It is fun, and it is the essence of play.

> Learning by doing refers to a theory of education expounded by American philosopher John Dewey. It is a hands-on approach to learning, meaning students must interact with their environment to adapt and learn.

The digital life

I didn't grow up having to deal with digital concerns at all. We had an old-fashioned television, and we sat in the evening and watched something together as a family. That was it. No screens, no computers, no cellphones, no PlayStations, no internet, no TikTok, no nothing. There weren't many alternatives then and, therefore, a lot of time was spent socialising with friends physically. Times have changed, and now we are constantly flooded with virtual temptations. My daughters have grown up with it with me and their father at their side. We have learnt to sail the digital universe simultaneously – and they are far better at it than us today. We have talked about good and ethical digital behaviour, and we have sat with them, curious to understand what fascinated them while keeping them informed about risks and traps. They use it daily with confidence now where we still feel slightly alienated. But nevertheless, digital life is a new forum in which to play freely.

Today, your teenager cannot be anywhere without a phone in hand, in their pocket, or on the table next to them. It has become their most loyal companion, and here they create relationships with the people around them. Every minute they risk someone texting with things they have to deal with, and here they are updated on what is happening, why, and how they perceive themselves. They navigate safely while engaging in many conversations at once and cannot imagine a non-digital life. Bored is so last year now that they feel energetic and intoxicated by the many opportunities their phone offers them. They are not stressed; they are alive. At least that's what they like to believe.

But you know better. This is what you tell your teen when they cannot get off their phone or out of bed. You want them to go out and get some fresh air, play football, or socialise with their friends instead of being preoccupied with whatever they are doing online. You remember a time before smartphones when your free time was your own, when it was used to process impressions and give your mind a break. However, the small spaces of 'free play' have disappeared, and it affects the well-being of your teenager. You have read the numbers and know that a high degree of phone use can lead to stress due to its ubiquitous availability. It can affect your teen's mental health and their sleep and physical health in the long run.

In Denmark, 97 out of 100 families have internet access at home. In the US, the percentage of families with internet access is around 96 per cent, and in the UK almost 95 per cent of the population were using the internet in 2020. That says something about our teens' easy access to the virtual paradise and that it is not only them who may be deeply dependent; we are too.

With regard to cellphones, 96 per cent of people in Denmark own one, 95 per cent of those in the US have one and in the UK 79 million mobile phone subscriptions are registered, interesting when you consider the current population is 67 million. Overall, China and India have the highest numbers of cellphone users, according to the World Population Review in 2021.

In the US, 75.4 per cent of people consider themselves addicted to their phones, in the UK it is 46 per cent, while in Denmark, every fourth adult feels highly or very highly dependent on their mobiles. However, to me, it seems like we do not differ much around the world – the digital world has sneaked into all of our everyday lives and therefore should have, more or less, the same positive or negative effects.

When it comes to adolescents, Danish teenagers spend an average of five hours on their mobile phones a day. In the UK it is 6.5 hours, while American teenagers spend up to 7 hours and 22 minutes a day – this amount of screen time does not include time spent on schoolwork. When adding in activities such as reading books and listening to music, the number jumped to 9 hours and 49 minutes, according to a 2019 report by Common Sense Media, a nonprofit organisation that promotes safe technology and media for children. It seems like a lot of time to me, and I can't stop thinking about how this affects them when compared to what I did with the many hours, not having access to any digital platforms as a teenager myself. What comes to me first is playing cards. Friends came by, and we drank tea and played cards forever in the afternoon and evenings during the week. Secondly, I read a lot of books. At one time I had read all the books from the shelves in my nearby library. Yes, the times have definitely changed.

I always try to look at my own behaviour in relation to what I expect from my daughters, and when I look at the numbers, I'm embarrassed to admit that today I am not always a good example in that area either; posting on Instagram every day as well as reading the newspaper or updating myself on friends and colleagues on LinkedIn. With so many adults addicted to their phones, I encourage you to look inward before scolding your teen for being the only one who has a problem.

According to Anne Eskerod Borgstrøm from Insight Manager, three media platforms in particular play a significant role in teenagers' daily digital communications. One is Snapchat, where they interact freely, just like in a class, which is the most direct reflection of reality. The second is Facebook, but they don't tend to use it that actively – mostly to get messages from the football or dance coach, and that sort of thing. From a teenage point of view, Facebook is primarily adult-driven communication. Third, Instagram is a popular platform to get inspiration and to stage themselves. Here they follow each other, but there is no possibility of direct conversation as in Snapchat. This is where they show their perfect selves, which they are very aware of. TikTok is gaining interest as well, with a billion users in 2021.

It is a sad fact that many teenagers prefer to be alone in their rooms to stay in contact with several Snapchat groups at the same time. That way they can follow and respond to everyone, being sure not to be excluded from social contexts. They have grown up to think that a world without social media seems impossible because there is too much to lose. This is a sad trend, as they also miss the close and deep real-world relationships that give them more meaningful satisfaction than the superficial digital ones can. Only 7 per cent of 15-year-old Danish girls and 13 per cent of 15-year-old boys frequently spend physical time with friends after school, which is worrying as they need physical contact to truly mirror themselves with their friends. Teenagers often choose to do what is easy and accessible and which gives them an immediate sense of satisfaction. They have no idea of long-term effects, and they don't give a thought about them. The consequences of not being online matter more. I hope that in the future they will be able to learn to handle their need to be on social media – and here, you as a parent are more than necessary.

Every time your teen posts a photo on Facebook or Instagram, writes a comment, or does a status update they share information with their friends. However, it is not only their friends who benefit from this information. Many companies are also interested in knowing what they like. Firms can use that information to target their advertisements. When your teen 'likes' a page, they implicitly allow the company behind it to post on their page, thus advertising and encouraging them to buy its products. Many teens know this well but do not find it worrisome – I am a little more sceptical because when Facebook or Google tries to figure out what your teen likes, there is a risk that they will only be presented with one-sided comments and articles that do not promote a view of a nuanced world. Fortunately, various features can limit the sharing of information, but this too is something teens must learn because otherwise they can have some long-term regrets.

Being constantly 'on' and engaged is stressful and because many teens are big consumers of digital social media, they feel the pressure it causes. The first thing they do in the morning on waking up is to check their phone and see what has come in during the night. It is also the last thing to check before falling asleep at night. Many even sleep with the sound on, so they wake up every time a new message is received. This is very disturbing for a good night's sleep and doesn't give their minds a break to find peace.

Suppose you want your teens to detox from their phones and create new free play habits (perhaps along with yourself). In that case, you have to ask them what they get from spending so much time on Snapchat, TikTok and Instagram and what is happening inside them when they can barely sleep because they have not posted their 44 streaks. You must address and talk about what is at stake for your teenager. Although it is not rational, most teenagers will very quickly feel as if they are missing out on conversations and updates, thereby positioning themselves as being incomprehensible and not included in the community. Either they are inside the fellowship or outside it, alone. It can feel like it is a matter of survival, which you can't just ignore. You can ask yourself, how much do your teens use their phones? Do they seem addicted in any way? Do you feel that screens take up too much of the time you have together with them? Do you understand their world?

If you choose to introduce screen rules, it is a good idea to explain why and be very aware of what you are taking from them. My argument has always been that the brain needs a break at night to be fresh and rested for the day to come. It made good sense for my kids, aiming to find a balance they could accept. Until they started high school as 17-year-olds, we had an agreement that they left their phones in the kitchen at night. This is how we had always prioritised things – just as I still do. Getting a good night's sleep has always been a priority. However, now they keep their phones on silent at night and deliberately put them down when ready to sleep. Since I am self-employed, I sit a lot at my computer when not counselling families. At times, it is almost around the clock, and I am not fully present unless I actively decide to put the work away for a while. So I am not much better myself! On the other hand, my phone is always on silent and is on the kitchen table. I am terrible at answering text messages. After being stressed by work pressure, I am conscious of taking it easy in that area. I am enormously conscientious, which makes me want to react right away and do what is expected. But I know I don't work well when I have to divide my attention between many fragmented areas, so I try to avoid it. This is how I try to take care of myself, and even though it may not always fit into others' pace, it has helped me to be more in the now and reduce my need to always be available.

The reality is that screen time can lead to addiction, and the body and mind will gradually change. What used to be a happy and curious teen with a zest for life can suddenly transform into a moody, aggressive and short-tempered one, withdrawing from social events, leading to a downward spiral which can be challenging to turn around. There are screen addictions and then, specifically, there is addiction to gaming, which is especially prevalent among teenage boys.

Gaming addiction grows slowly, as the brain's reward centre secretes the hormone dopamine, making your teen happy. Dopamine is activated when they get good grades, score a goal in football, climb high up in a tree, solve a task, or reach a new level on a computer game. It just feels good, so you do not always see it affecting them right away. When it hits, you will know. You will feel powerless and without any tools to handle their aroused behaviour. Gaming slowly takes over your teen's dopamine system, and the brain will be flooded with the hormone. As a response, the brain begins to down-regulate its sensitivity to dopamine. And that means that ordinary everyday experiences, which previously made your teen happy and satisfied, suddenly feel inadequate, and it will be the computer game that now determines what satisfies the brain. That is why many teens can't find any motivation to do something other than gaming as it doesn't feel as exhilarating.

Another side effect is that gaming has a magnetic attraction. Because the brain is accustomed to its reward, it automatically responds to the expectation of an early reward when the teenager encounters something in school, with friends, in the supermarket that can be linked to the computer game. The teen's thoughts will constantly circle to return to the game. It is like when you decide not to eat sugar or sweets, but you can't stop thinking about it.

And finally, since the brain is elastic, it only develops those areas that are used and therefore not all its areas. This means that some areas dwindle while others are being strengthened. However, some basic regions are being developed as a child. These are language, motor skills, movement, and social contact with other people. When teenagers play a lot on screens, they do not get trained in these areas. They are often only repeating their own pattern in themselves – if it becomes more than two hours of screen time a day.

If certain brain areas are not trained, it may inhibit the brain's impulse control of the emotional response. It simply becomes a vicious circle because your teen will find it hard to respond to challenges and unable to control their temper. After a tantrum – yes, that still happens – they often get upset because they do not understand why they reacted so strongly.

You must remember that adolescence should be full of many different aspects of experimentation and playing freely; teenagers should not only be allowed to sit in front of a screen, because that is what they want. Teens need fresh air and light and should never be isolated from the outer world. It won't do them any good in the long run. They need to socialise and connect with other people. They need to face the challenges life throws at them. They need to go out in nature, mingle, and join in some fun activities, aka duties. They need to feel that they matter, and they can only do that if they are around their family, friends and community, getting wiser about who they are.

I am certain that there is too much pressure on teens today, making it even more important to help them find a healthy digital balance. Even if they are 'digital natives', it doesn't mean that they are born with the ability to control what they do, just as they are not born with the ability to control how many sweets they can eat when they walk into a sweetshop. It is something that we must teach them, and it requires that you familiarise yourselves with their world and understand what is to be gained or lost for them. Enter a dialogue, ask when it makes sense to put their phone away. It can be when you have a time of togetherness – to *hygge* – every time you eat, or when you sleep, then you do not have the phone lying in front of you. You must prioritise physical presence. It is a great way to show your teenager that it makes sense to put their phone down while they feel greater inner well-being which lowers stress and loneliness. Digital education does not come by itself; it comes from you leading the way.

Courage

Courage is the cousin of hope and is very closely related to the zone of proximal development. Courage and hope are connected because there is an implicit hope in daring to do something, achieve something, or create something. Courage means to explore new territory, and teenagers do this all the time. Like when my eldest daughter travelled to Africa to teach as a volunteer at a school in Zambia. Or, while she was there in Zambia, when she threw herself off the bridge over Victoria Falls in a bungee jump. Or when she stood in front of many students as a 19-year-old substitute teacher at our local school. This is courage, but courage is also found in the small, almost invisible everyday events such as being open and available to people, contacting a distant friend, or taking a leap of faith and saying yes to something you've longed for.

This is also a way of playing freely. Think about what courage it takes when teenagers enter new social relationships. There is a lot to be won or lost, and they may risk losing face and being rejected. Yet it happens all the time. Precisely the same as when you first balance over a tree trunk as a child, you risk falling or others being faster and better than you, but you dare the attempt. Now you dare all the time as a teenager, sometimes with a helping hand from an adult, many times not. Although they do not always succeed, teenagers bring courage to their attempts to develop themselves.

Courage is also when your teenager stands up and argues for their views or values. You regard them as being nosy and disrespectful. No, they are brave, because trying and testing everything they absorb from their friends and surroundings will only make them wiser about themselves. It is healthy, and although it may irritate you, you must learn to understand what is going on with them. Often they do not know it themselves; it can feel almost vital, a compulsion. But you can better meet them with empathy when you understand the underlying reason. Some years ago, I had a boy in therapy. He was introduced to me because he had tried to take his own life several times but did not want psychiatric treatment. His family did not talk about emotions but focused on high grades and academia that did not suit his personality. He cut himself and was quiet with his pain when he did not run away from home for several days.

Sometimes it happens that you feel wrongly placed in your own family. In Denmark, we have a saying that slightly negatively expresses that you are the black sheep in the family, who stands out from the norm; the one who learns to adapt but never feels seen and loved for who they are. It can be unreasonably challenging to live in a way where your whole self – your entire starry sky – is not accepted and where you cannot recognise yourself in those on whom you depend.

This beautiful young man had a primordial force inside that longed for life. He worked for some time to build up his own sense of identity and be independent of his family. At the same time, he became clearer about who he was and dared to go his own way in the world. His behaviour was not sensational or different, but he broke with a family structure that was not healthy for him and managed to rise from the depths – not as an angry young man, but as a strengthened and independent one who could stand by the life choices he needed to make. Sometimes life goes this way, and this beautiful soul did not give up but found the courage to create the life he had dreamt of.

Your teen is also brave when they dare to be vulnerable, especially in a world that calls for a certain kind of hardness. There is so much that they try to live up to, whether it is beauty ideals, good grades, many 'likes', or social inclusion; vulnerability is a strength.

I admire those who dare to open up and share their worries, confusions and uncertainties. It makes them, in my eyes, unique role models because it breeds a sense of redemption and intimacy that spreads to others. Of course, it requires an atmosphere where it is safe for this to be possible. Sometimes in my consultations I come across young people who are very lonely. They have no one to go to but they are stronger than many others as they allow themselves to feel the vulnerable sides of themselves, which is admirable. I have always taught my daughters that it is essential to mark and share their thoughts with either of us, their parents, or good and close friends. Not everyone has known how to meet this vulnerability, but the vast majority have reacted by opening up and daring to be vulnerable and exposed themselves. Trust creates trust. Courage generates more courage.

Courage is also when your teenager tests themselves and become wiser about what is not for them. Yes, they drink alcohol and go to parties, and maybe weed is smoked. There are kisses, and boundaries are experimented with and subsequently defined. There is laughter and crying, friendships disappear, and new ones are added. The norms and values instilled through childhood are tested, and some persist while others acquire new dimensions. It is life as a teenager and life as a parent of teens.

Let us look on our teens as brave, with everything they throw themselves into and everything they learn and cultivate. It is absolutely crazy how much courage being a teenager requires. The courage that holds together with hope and faith is what keeps it all running just as it should, contributing to building independence and character which makes stronger and confident human beings.

CHAPTER 5

Formation

DANISH *EFTERSKOLES*

Have you ever heard of *efterskoles*? A word which, if you split it in two, means 'after school'. 'Should we make an appointment after school?' Or, 'What are you going to do after school?' Well, in this case it is not a request but a place to go and have the time of your life – playing freely. Not many know of these unique Danish independent residential schools for students between 14 and 18 years old, where at this moment almost 40 per cent of all Danish students attend for either one, two, or three years.

The word *efterskole* literally translates to 'after school' in English but is often used in reference to an independent boarding school, which isn't quite right. The Danish–English dictionaries offer 'continuation school', which also is a misleading description of the *efterskole*'s purpose and form. Therefore, I will use *efterskole* or *efterskoles* (in the plural) for this special Danish place for teenagers to join.

If your child attends an *efterskole*, you can be sure that either their parents joined one or at least they know of someone who also had the experience themselves. Both my sisters did it many years ago, and children of friends, colleagues and neighbours in my inner circle have done it too. I didn't at the time I had the opportunity, but later on, when I graduated, I went to a youth folk high school for one year, which is similar to an *efterskole*, just without any exams. My daughters were given the same opportunity, but neither of them had the desire to try it out. They both wanted to go directly to college without taking a break from the ordinary school system.

For many, though, the tradition passes from generation to generation, if the teenager wants to go. The social authorities also send some vulnerable students to give them a year of growth in a safe and secure environment. You will never find a place that embraces all aspects of life and all kinds of people in such a fine and concentrated manner while you are still growing. Teenagers live and welcome the beautifully authentic now without recognising the long-term influence these memories and experiences have on them, which makes the spirit of *efterskoles* extremely welcoming.

The why

What *efterskoles* offer is a bit of the adult life that awaits, as you come to live with strangers away from familiar and safe surroundings. *Efterskole* means learning new sides of yourself, dyeing your hair green, leaving your bra off, cleaning with friends, being on food teams, and singing hymns. *Efterskole* is music, sport, theatre, nature and art. *Efterskole* is to endure homesickness, get a BFF, and fall in love for the first time. *Efterskole* is to laugh, cry, rejoice and be challenged. *Efterskole* is full of togetherness, free play and life wisdom, all consumed with Crystal Maggie dice that cannot be found elsewhere. Prejudices are broken down, and self-worth, self-confidence and self-esteem are increased in the best way possible.

It sounds like a utopia, but, of course, it isn't. Every teenager has a different experience, as life also can feel challenging when the joy and excitement fade after a while as daily routines knock on the door, as they do everywhere. Still, this is a part of the expected journey that belongs to living at an *efterskole*. You can't flee from facing the girl who ignores you, and you have to come to classes and do your homework. The teachers at *efterskoles* are prepared and have dedicated their professional lives to coping with all the small and more significant ups and downs that arise for their students, both internal and external. There will always be some of different maturity levels; some will need the closeness and comfort of an adult presence while others function perfectly on their own. Therefore, one of the unique things about the *efterskole* is the teacher–student relationship. The teachers are responsible for teaching and for student supervision outside school hours. This means that teachers and students are together the whole day, from when they wake up until they go to bed. No student will ever be left alone if there is a need for support, assistance, or just a hug. This often engenders a close, personal and informal relationship between them, with teachers becoming essential and significant role models.

Teenagers of today

Nowadays, children are born into a time of opportunity, coupled with a performance society. They can 'become anything, as long as they want it enough'. Therefore, it is not unusual for many adolescents to blame themselves when they experience not succeeding. Suppose they feel they have all the opportunities that time allows and still fail. In that case, they blame themselves and point fingers inwardly if, for example, they don't do well in school and get good grades and the appropriate recognition they strive for. And if you *are* nothing, you become *nothing*. That is a lot of pressure to carry on a young growing teenager's shoulders. Therefore, many struggle with anxiety and loneliness, and have suicidal thoughts; unfortunately, they often have no one to go to. That is a huge problem that needs to be addressed.

I especially like the way *efterskoles* counter this pressure, because it is unthinkable to keep a mask on for a very long time. Eventually it will fall off and the naked, authentic person will stand there, vulnerable and easy to chase. But that doesn't happen – the opposite will. As elaborated in *The Danish Way of Parenting*, a feeling of *togetherness* occurs, and a sense of pure acceptance spreads around everyone. Isn't that what you wish for your teenager – to feel whole and accepted? I know for me it is; I want my children's starry sky to shine fully. Because they weren't interested in attending an *efterskole*, we went as a family to summer folk high school for three years – all four of us. I thought my daughters should feel the unique atmosphere and diversity, similar to *efterskoles*, and meet committed and dedicated teachers, a place with lots of enduring Danish values similar to those inherited values I was raised with.

One year at *efterskole* is a life experience that will never appear on a diploma and cannot be used as a punchline on a CV or job application. But in a world where children are made into small adults early, with little space to play and where everything else must preferably be measurable and evaluated, experiences and memories are much more important than this, in my opinion. *Efterskoles* facilitate a free space where the outside world is on hold, where it is OK to live and flourish at an age-appropriate pace, and where such a year becomes the first taste of freedom and independence – step by step. Some even state playfully that a year at *efterskole* equates to seven human years because of its enormous social, emotional and educational impact.

The founding of *efterskoles*

Efterskoles have not come about by chance. Their founding was based on a pedagogical need, which requires 'a school after one's normal schooling'. A school form which, through education, enlightenment and democracy, contributes to a shared existence and social cohesion within society. The Executive Order on *Efterskoles* and Free Vocational Schools states that: 'The *efterskole* shall contribute to enlightenment for life, general education and democratic citizenship.' At the same time, the Executive Order clarifies that the *efterskole*'s task is educational in general, as well as the broader task of supporting students' character formation.

Historically and culturally, the first *efterskole* was founded about 150 years ago. The schools were closely related to the Danish Folk High School, and the educational ideas of N. F. S. Grundtvig (1783–1872), a minister, writer and poet who wanted schools to provide enlightenment for life rather than formal vocational training. But it was a teacher, Christen Kold (1816–70), who most notably transformed Grundtvig's visionary ideas into educational practice.

While Grundtvig intended the *folkehøjskoles* (folk high schools) to be for adults, Kold wanted to reach young people when they entered puberty. Thus Kold's first school, founded at Ryslinge in 1851, was for young farmhands, and this school is recognised as the first *efterskole*. A famous anecdote concerns how Kold met a young farmhand out in the fields and tried to persuade him to come to his *efterskole*. When asked what good it would do a future farmer, Kold asked him if he had a pocket watch. Yes, he had. 'That watch,' said Kold, 'can go for a time, and then it has to be wound up again, but at my school, you will be wound up so that you will never stop!'

Formation

Formation most often refers to being an (educated) and insightful human being who, with sufficient autonomy, will lead himself and others towards being able to make valuable and wise decisions. To realise this ideal, the school and education system has historically been assigned a unique role in this formation process, and the same goes for *efterskoles*.

Formation for me is to become familiar with our history, norms and cultural traditions, advantages and disadvantages, with the hope that we will one day choose these values ourselves because we *want* to and not because we will be rewarded for our choice or punished for not choosing it. Formation is to learn self-direction and to develop the power to make our own choices without depending on our parents or teachers. To do that, we must cultivate critical thinking, and we must have the mindset of 'I am the owner too', whether at home or in the classroom. In other words, your teenager needs an inner grounding (autonomy). Otherwise, they cannot become independent because they will constantly be looking to what their friends are doing. That is, they will become the externally controlled teenager who is continually looking around a large circle to find out what 'I' should take cues from. Unlike your inner controlled teenager, who has a point of view, some values, and some internal norms that formation should basically provide, whether at home or from the educational system around the teen.

Nurturing this formation process at *efterskoles* or in the

ordinary school system is done in collaboration with the other students. Everyone must try to contribute equally and feel shared responsibility when placed in teams to do chores and tasks to optimise daily life. This only succeeds when they feel committed and respect each other and each other's point of view. Formation is about listening to others with curiosity and respect and taking a critical stand on what is presented, as it is wise to not take everything for granted. A premise for formation is that routines or common practices must be learnt as a necessary foundation for everyone to be able to free themselves from the rules and finally choose democracy on an enlightened basis. The formation process is to be found everywhere at *efterskoles*, and in the Danish educational system in general.

Efterskoles through parents' lenses

Why are Danish parents willing to let go of their teenagers at such a sensitive time? Shouldn't we keep our teenagers close to make sure they don't rebel? What if they get influenced negatively by someone with values different from theirs, or none at all? What if it means losing the precious contact built up since they were little? What if we can't recognise our child when they return home?

So much fear and distrust are normal when not knowing what to expect from the future, and you feel you must hold on and never lose control of what might be best for the child. And you know why? It is because these thoughts are all about *you*. It isn't fair turning off stars on behalf of your teenager because of something that awakens your extinguished stars. Remember that it is *they* who are practising to fly, a skill which you have taught them to master for so many years. Therefore, in this moment you must ask yourself: 'What is it that controls my thoughts right now? Am I acting unconsciously or consciously? How can I take "time out" to calm my nervous system? How can I allow my child's starry sky to shine fully?' Herein lies the characteristics of being free and the importance of play.

Leaving your child at *efterskoles* is to leave the little control you have at the door and trust in the development process your teenager needs to experience on their own. It also allows a part of you to be healed. Most Danish parents generally find that their child is stronger, academically, personally and socially, after a stay at *efterskole*. Overall, the combination of academical, personal and socially unique development about the *efterskole* stay is the essence of the experience. This development is essential for your teenager's future education and career, making parents welcome their children's participation with great expectations and joy.

Much is done to ensure that the collaboration between school and parents works optimally. Conversations are held with the student and their parents during the year. Parents are invited to events, and events without parental interaction are posted on social media. All questions are welcome, and an open and positive dialogue is constantly being prioritised. Mutual trust from both sides is the key. Like when your toddler climbs a tree trunk and you show that you have confidence that your child can master this new step, you also have trust in the world that unfolds freely under safe cirstumstances for your teenager now.

It is not a bargain

A year at *efterskole* isn't mandatory, nor is it free to attend, like schools usually are in Denmark, even though it would be fantastic for everyone if it were. A year at *efterskole* costs around £13,500 or $16,000 – which, if you are not a Danish citizen, must be paid upfront. For Danes, the expense is dependent on the parents' income, but everyone receives some state support. As *efterskoles* are independent, or 'free schools', they can set the price themselves depending on the facilities and activities offered. This means that there can be a big difference in price depending on where you send your teenager. However, this does not necessarily say anything about the quality, as there are bigger and smaller *efterskoles* that have different opportunities and cater for different needs.

I have had several clients in my practice who seriously struggle with their lives. They have had significant value from a year at *efterskole*. They had no parents to give them this chance to blend in with more fortunate teenagers. However, the Danish system works so that if you can't afford it yourself, there are still equal opportunities for everyone. The municipalities concerned with these young people can provide a place for them and either share the bill with the *efterskole* or pay the total amount. Denmark is a welfare society where this is possible and an essential part of our democratic foundation where this character formation is highly valued. The percentage of those students is small, but they are present every year.

The Danish welfare society is something that many Danes take for granted but it defines Denmark. The total welfare model is expensive (estimated at $88 billion a year), but, in return, it creates security and opportunities for people here. We all have free access to hospitals and education, and everyone is supported to avoid ending up in deep poverty. Welfare has been a continued contributor to Denmark being one of Europe's (and one of the world's) most equal societies.

Translating the formation process into everyday life

Formation is not only something that appears in a year at *efterskole*; it grows through everyday practices in the family and where your individual footprints are set. Formation occurs in ways small and big: when talking about the day and reflecting on your own and others' behaviour. When reading books that give historical perspectives and cultural dimensions. When teaching your teen to distinguish between reality and fantasy. When educating them in online ethics and behaviour. When you teach them not to believe everything they read – that there are first-hand descriptions, second-hand, third-hand, etc. When you show care and consideration, openness and generosity. When you are kind to strangers and help without expecting anything in return. When you trust your teens and back up their dreams. When you let them recognise themselves, and endeavour to make your shared relationship respectful and loving. Formation is both conscious and unconscious, but you can focus on it if you want your teens to develop into self-thinking individuals who will risk standing up for themselves in a healthy and sustainable way in this diverse and sometimes uncertain world.

The relationship between parents is one of the family bonds that significantly impacts the family's overall quality of life, and if there are conflicts there they affect everyone, and the energy in the home feels insecure. After all, you and your partner's way of being together is your teenager's most important role model for social behaviour and dealing with emotions. Therefore, your relationship with your partner or spouse is vital for the security of your teen's upbringing and emotional development. At the same time, it is also important for you to thrive in the family. Not all conflicts can be avoided, of course. It is important to emphasise that if they are resolved constructively and followed up by reconciliation, parental arguments can also be an excellent example for the teen about their own way of dealing with conflicts in the future.

Formation takes place all the time and is something that is mainly subconscious for Danes. Still, it is clear that if you want to stay focused on a positive character education for your teen, then it requires that you as a parent are in a place in life where there is room and energy to act by your norms and values. This is not always the case. Therefore, it is positive to know that formation is ubiquitous in Danish schools and educational institutions, written into the various school acts to ensure that all adolescents receive it there to a greater or lesser degree.

The word is spreading

In South Korea, they have opened their eyes to the Danish model of *efterskoles*, led by Mr Oh Yeon-ho, an author, entrepreneur and journalist who believed that getting to know the philosophy behind Danish *efterskoles* is key to understanding Danish democracy, Danish companies, and Danish culture – and why Denmark has been voted the happiest country in the world for so many years. He found that the secret of a happy Danish society is closely related to a happy education. He wanted to learn all about Danish culture, forest kindergartens, folk high schools and *efterskoles*, so he set up a delegation of educators, investors and students to delve into Denmark's pedagogical principles, visiting Denmark 23 times since 2013. What fascinated him especially was the right to look at things differently and not follow the stream and conventional ideas of educating.

Mr Oh wants children and young people in South Korea to develop into active citizens who can take care of their own lives in the wider community, as he has seen in Denmark. Therefore, he first founded one *efterskole*, Ggumtle, where students participated from all areas of South Korea. As he is such a strong believer in the vision of changing the circumstances for the youth in his country, his newest project has been to create an entire movement based on the pedagogical thoughts from Denmark on one of the Korean islands. Here is an *efterskole*, a free school, a folk high school, and an educational institution for teachers based on Denmark's knowledge, inspiration and experience. The money he earns from giving lectures goes to fund these projects, which makes him even more of a star in my eyes.

Mr Oh's hard work in bringing the Danish *efterskole* tradition, with its utterly unique combination of professionalism and community, to South Korea earned him the N. F. S. Grundtvig Prize in 2018 for being visible proof that Grundtvig's thoughts on school and society extend far beyond Denmark's borders. This is such excellent news, and if Mr Oh's visionary ambitions could spread even more, there is a hope that we will slowly raise new generations with the ability to think for themselves and make decisions based on their own needs, who can communicate and accept themselves in a diverse world, which in the long run will give them greater satisfaction and more comprehensive happiness.

Since 2014 Mr Oh has given more than 1,400 lectures on Grundtvig, Denmark, and *efterskoles*. He has written a book, *Can We Also Be Happy?*, about Denmark, Grundtvig, and the Danish school system, including teachers' education, which has sold more than 100,000 copies.

I have been honored to meet and talk with Mr Oh. When I asked him about what in his eyes makes Denmark unique when it comes to children and their well-being, he told me that it is due to our freedom of choice that makes children independent regardless of their parents or the existing order of society. There are many good routes to go in life, so the competition is not fierce, he explains. He also points out that all children in school are allowed to participate even if they are not great or the best in class. This means that students with excellent grades are not the only ones who have a presence – and such an atmosphere allows 'you to love yourself'. I love that angle, and since I find his wisdom unique, I asked him to give parents from all over the world one piece of advice, to which he replied:

> Life keeps growing all the time. The reason why growing children sometimes get nervous is that they have the idea that *my grades, my appearance, and my personality, my life have already been decided.* Going beyond this determinism requires adult models. Even when parents reach their forties or fifties, if they are curious about new things and develop themselves, their children will also imitate them. When parents are excited, play and live for the day, the children will also live the same life. Isn't the greatest gift a parent can give to a child that *Life is worth living*!?

With this, let us embrace that your teenager learns to solve problems, relates to other people, learns about boundaries and become clearer about what feels good or bad. They become self-directed, learn know how to think critically, and love themselves for who they are when embracing the characteristics of playing freely at the stage they are at.

CHAPTER 6

Togetherness

GRASPING THE SOCIAL LANGUAGE

The social aspect of life exploded when I became a teenager. A world suddenly opened, as if I had found the door to the secret treasury I had heard about since I was a child but had never had the navigation equipment to find. It was wild, intense and fun. I did not recall approaching teenagerhood for years before; there were only fleeting sensations that something was happening to my body and interests. Then **BOOM!** I had become a teenager. Not a pre-teenager or tween, but a full-blown teen ready to take in all the good stuff from life with my friends – and no longer with my family.

Adolescence is about the natural transition that occurs from being family-centred to becoming friend- or me-centred. As a parent you stop being your teens' go-to person as friendships become increasingly significant and social skills are practised when mirroring peers. It is when your teen learns to read and understand themselves and others and interact with people who are not already familiar. They discover that they are not alone and that their friends feel the same emotions, insecurities, fears and anxieties; therefore, they realise that their feelings are normal and expected. This is a natural and necessary phase, but at the same time, as a parent it can appear challenging, suddenly to feel ignored or abandoned in favour of friends whose opinions and attitudes gain far greater value when it comes to decisions, character and affection than yours. But watching them chatting and laughing with each other is sweet and so life-affirming, remembering how this unique atmosphere in a bubble of happiness feels.

> Hygge has a unique invisible energy that is rooted in a shared desire to be together, like a state of mind where you feel connected, filled with closeness and shared values all combined into a more prominent feeling of togetherness.

The landscape is changing

Concentrating on keeping a close and meaningful relationship, with awareness and insight into what is 'under construction', is perhaps one of the most important aspects of being a parent to a teenager. The bond between you is the key to everything. This can be tested to the extreme, especially with a teenager's sometimes unreasonable behaviour, but never lose faith in its value. You will be put on the sidelines because your teen needs to connect with their friends and form their character. But it is not to be taken personally.

Instead, you can concede this important time and continue to build on a good, welcoming and confidential connection with them. Let home be their safe place, where everything they pick up from friends and their surroundings is set up against the set of values that bind your family together. The place where they can allow themselves to feel what matters to them, letting their guard down. The place that ensures many stars in their sky stay on no matter the social customs and friends' codes. This works best if you are free of prejudice and curious about what they share with you. If you are available when they need a shoulder, listen and let them feel their emotions without trying to fix things immediately. If you embrace them and don't scold or start an argument if they behave annoyingly. Instead, treat their trust in you with care and thoughtfulness instead of letting your anxiety or irritation flow over them when they come home too late.

My awareness has continually been on this, and I have focused on being my daughters' place to go day and night – always ready to listen. We sometimes go on short weekend trips or for a walk, just two of us, play cards, watch TV, eat good food, or *hygge* in the cottage – a place that welcomes relaxation, slowness, peace and togetherness, where our dog walks and nips berries from the bushes and where my daughters lie on the sofa reading books, interrupted only by yatzy or who's going to the seaside for a swim. A sanctuary for me and my family, it's a place that strengthens the relationship I have with each of them, allowing us the time to tune into each other without any interruptions. I also make sure to check in with them daily (Ida has moved away from home now, so it is done a little differently with her). I do this by hearing about their day, looking them in the eye, and letting them know – without words – that I see them, while making myself available if I sense some kind of emotional imbalance. But knowing their friends, inviting them for dinner and respecting their friendships is also key.

I remind myself that I am just a background figure, which to start with wasn't easy to do but feels right now I really understand what it means. Never an indifferent background figure, but the most important kind that makes healthy detachment possible without passing on guilt to my girls. In particular, avoiding falling into the trap that our teenagers must be close to us to meet our need for presence instead of their need for freedom and independence. This is an important phase for them where friends are of high value.

You are their safe haven, from where they sail every day out on the great sea, which can be quiet or in revolt. Still, they come back when the day is over and need to be refuelled mentally and physically with safe background figures that trust in them. No matter how vital your teens' friends are, the significance of their relationship with you should never be overlooked.

Moving mountains

'Make some friends; why is it that hard for you!' 'Suck it up and do like the others!' 'She ignores you; what don't you get?' We can be harsh with our teenagers when they do not know what we spent many years understanding ourselves. And which hits a sore spot – perhaps an extinguished star – in us.

Nothing is as painful as experiencing that life is a little more difficult for your teen than you had hoped for. Now that you have learnt to interpret the social rules in the tremendous social whirlwind, your teenager should be able to as well. BUT, reading and understanding the many different ways of communicating, accompanied by an explosive blast of implicit expectations and norms, much pressure from social media, and the change in the narrative of online friendships' superficial power, is more than hard in adolescence. This journey needs to have been worked on from childhood, where you teach your children to read facial expressions. How to look when angry, sad, happy, fearful, etc., and how the body is used to communicate nonverbally. Many studies have investigated how much of communication is nonverbal; in reality, the answer isn't all that cut-and-dried. Everyone does agree that it makes up a huge part, however, which highlights the need to learn to decode it.

This is a cardinal point in my work with the European Erasmus+ scheme, to implement the teaching of empathy in primary schools' curricula in Europe. The Erasmus+ general objective is to support, through lifelong learning, the educational, professional and personal development of people in education, training, youth and sports, in Europe and beyond, thereby contributing to sustainable growth, quality jobs and social cohesion, to driving innovation, and to strengthening European identity and active citizenship.

Too many children grow up without their empathetic abilities nurtured, which causes distance and a more unloving attitude among everyone. Of course, they have to learn to decode where they are in the social hierarchy and deal with not necessarily being at the top. Still, they also must understand the many invisible and unspoken practices of being in a group of friends within their everyday lives. No wonder they can feel confused.

It can be challenging to master and understand those social languages when you are 5 years old, 15 or even 35, but as adults, you know it carries significant value to be a master at it. Therefore, you so much wish your teenager to grasp this part of life because you know it is essential for their well-being. You hope they will have friends and be a likable person. You hope that they will learn to regulate their own behaviour and develop empathy to understand their own feelings and their friends' feelings. You hope they will look at conflicts in a nuanced way, familiarise themselves with their friends' experiences, argue for their opinions, and find compromises in conflict situations. You hope they fall in love and join a healthy and caring community with many sparkling stars, much fun and togetherness. We have so many expectations on behalf of our teens.

Whether your teenager is impatient or careful, outgoing or introverted, their social skills are essential for taking the initiative and being curious and open while approaching their surroundings. This time of their life will undoubtedly contribute to insecurities and doubts along the way: 'Why am I a poor friend when I am not defending her attitude?' 'Why am I provocative when saying no, and why am I not allowed to kiss her when she seems interested?' Social practices are insanely tricky to manoeuvre in, but it is through taking actions that teens learn to make good decisions for themselves in a shared alliance with others.

A strong social network is one of the most significant factors in your overall happiness. Therefore, understanding what is up for grabs for your teen makes it even more critical that you support them in whatever they feel is suitable. They may turn left when you suggest right but let them figure out what gives them meaning and purpose with you having their back. This requires intense dedication, as most of us have felt not welcomed or included by others in the past, which has led to some survival strategies developing that you can easily throw onto your teenagers and turn off stars. Breathe deeply and give a warm hug to the 'little you' who was once hurt, before turning towards your teen confiding in you, and meeting them in their sorrow.

Wanting to live

One study, using data from a nationally illustrative sample of more than 111,000 adolescents, investigated whether teenagers in friendship networks had better mental health, as measured by several depressive symptoms. The findings made clear that teens with more friends had fewer symptoms of depression. In addition, teens with a friendship network felt a sense of belonging. As a result, those teens had more positive feelings about their relationships with other people in society. Moreover, studies also analysed how having a best friend influences mental health. The findings showed

that adolescent best friend attachment is linked to psychological health.

Teen friendship is so crucial that going without it hurts –
literally. A brain-imaging study at the University of Michigan
indicates that social rejection activates the same parts of the
brain as physical pain. Thus, teenagers being left out of a
group feel the rejection deeply and take it personally, and,
for many, this starts a spiral of self-blame. Friendships are
not only for fun, but they are also vital for life. As Dr Daniel
J. Siegel, a clinical professor of psychiatry, states:

> Why would it be natural to turn toward your peers as
> an adolescent? Because that's on whom you're going to
> depend on when you leave home. Often, in the wild, a
> mammal without an adolescent peer group is as good
> as dead. So connecting with a peer group can feel like a
> matter of survival.

There is no doubt that friendships are in high demand when
teenage life unfolds, which does not mean friendship exists
by itself. Jealousy, hierarchy – who is tallest, strongest, most
beautiful, has pubic hair – as well as social intelligence come
into play. Sometimes your teen is lucky to be in a class, or
activity group, or social circle that works well, and where it is
possible to build good healthy relationships without too many
ups and downs. Whether or not friendships will succeed is
difficult to determine in advance; is it common values that
bind young people together? Is it common interests, or are
they at about the same stage in terms of maturity? Maybe it

is a mix of all these things, but trust must be the starting point for friendships to work optimally, with depth and closeness.

Trust must, however, sometimes be put to the side, such as when it is not being excluded from those at the top of the hierarchy that matters most. Whether you acknowledge it or not, there is an unconscious sorting in who automatically becomes the leader, the one that the others would like to lean on. Therefore, in friendship constellations it is crucial that a person can be a healthy role model for the rest of the group, rather than someone who uses an unconscious strategy such as bullying. My experience is that many teens are willing to compromise on values like loyalty, decency and being a good friend to not be the person who risks becoming the object of humiliation and exclusion from the community. The survival of the fittest, as Darwin put it; better stay neutral and say nothing (even if that is to choose sides) in order to remain in the group, to seek closeness by avoiding standing out. What many don't grasp is that Darwin meant that those who learn to adjust to fit in, survive.

The closest I have felt to being completely powerless was a period when my daughter was sad for the sole reason that she did not buy into peer pressure but continued to be true to herself and the values she stands for – kindness, openness, and the gift to see the best in others – although some girls' jealousy around her was all-consuming and intimidating. Sometimes girls can be malicious once they become rivals, primarily through the use of nonverbal language, which makes up 80 per cent of our communication; girls are experts in rolling eyes and ignoring. There is nothing new in this; we know from ourselves that our most primitive survival strategies come to life if we feel threatened in any social contexts we move in. Still, there is a limit to how much we can take. I could stand and watch from the outside as my daughter's joy disappeared without being able to do anything, as she refused to follow in their footsteps and respond with rage or bitterness. When things are tough, we tend to lose perspective. We can get caught up in the situation and not keep track of what is going on inside us or what our responses to the external situation are. That can feed the situation so it gets out of control. But my daughter is beautiful and remarkably powerful in a sensitive way, so every day she faced the bullies with head held high but mentally deflated when she got home, despairing and unhappy that she had done nothing wrong but be herself. Clearly, we talked a lot about those who behave badly like that being the ones who are having a hard time, and since my daughter is hugely empathetic, she understood where their actions originated from and felt their pain. But, at the same time, she had to distance herself from them by putting up a shield to protect herself in order to function as well as possible, which was not easy.

There is so much anxiety over losing control of your teens' direction and knowing that it can either go wrong or turn out positively. In my case, I repeatedly told myself in that period that I shouldn't be worried and that the insight and learning my daughter would gain from this would be worth more than a bar of gold when she was on the other side of it. I knew she was OK at home and that she felt safe and had her family close. Still, I felt sore and down like never before, thinking that I couldn't alter the outside world (even though we tried all possible solutions) besides standing close at her side. Sore because something external was causing this pain in her, and down since I carried her sadness with me.

It was tough to witness her going through this time. Still, I knew she would find the strength within and rise from the gloom when she was ready, and then she would have acquired one of the most essential life lessons: that she will forever know where to find the power to manage life's valleys whenever they find their way to her fine soul. She did when the scenery around her changed, and it made her more resilient and capable than ever.

When facing challenging times it is always crucial to put into perspective and reflect on what happens when you end up in difficult, unshakable situations that cannot be fixed. Sometimes it takes two to tango, and sometimes it is only a solo move. Ironically, you can end up having to teach your children that not everyone wishes them well and that it may be necessary to be more resolute in their attitude, especially when you have teens with hearts as soft as butter. It hurts, especially when the most important thing for me is that my daughters grow up to be kind to others, empathetic and generous.

The anecdote above says something about the power of social construction and what is at stake for the individual's 'survival' during this critical period of our teens' lives. It sometimes costs that the healthy role model, who stands side by side with the tormentor in the hierarchy, becomes the target of everyone's sniping, without anyone daring to stand up for their friend, and thus becoming a co-bully because fear wins. This is a dynamic that is interesting, sad and incredibly difficult to handle.

It requires skilled teachers, coaches and present parents who can engage in honest dialogue around those who create this destructive dynamic. Many people are aware that if someone is dominating others through fear, they are having a hard time. Maybe the person comes from a home without love and parental presence that has cost them many extinguished stars. There is always a valid reason behind the way children, adolescents and adults behave, but it is not the same as saying that it is OK and that you must accept it.

'I feel left out' must always be taken seriously on our part. We wish we could control the world and point it in a better direction with deep and meaningful friendships; save your teens from the pain that they feel, and which awakens extinguished stars within us. Feeling connected to others is something Danes have always associated with meaning and purpose. We call it *hygge*. Without the synergy and comfort of others, we simply can't function well.

I think of Özlem Cekic, former Danish Member of Parliament, author and public debater who invites people to 'dialogue coffee meetings', where she meets with those who disagree with her for a mutually respectful conversation in private. It is not about reaching an agreement but rather an acceptance of the opposite view. It often ends up that despite their differences, they also find common ground. It is beautiful and the way forward for understanding and empathy, because, through sharing stories, you connect with others and gain new insights and new perspectives. When it comes to dealing with social exclusion or stopping bullying, schools must have a readiness to deal with this. This is partly the case in most places, but much is left to the parents. The effects of being laughed at, ignored, or humiliated are only expressed when teens feel secure. As much as teachers or parents aim to combat these effects, they can't change deep extinguished stars for those not close to them.

Being 'in the circle' or 'outside the circle' of friends is a condition in which your teenager constantly tries to manoeuvre. It is unbearable when faced with your teenager who struggles to hold on to their self-esteem and preserve their integrity and dignity while keeping a fragile identity. It brings out the worst instinctive forces within those of you who are watching this from the outside. You know that you can only support and help to a certain point, and must have confidence that time and a process like this is a powerful life experience, bringing much wisdom to be used in the future – while making sure that your teen's emotional cup is filled to the brim with love and your presence every single day.

Social hierarchy and friendships are not simply for fun. There is everything to gain and everything to lose, which is why it is such an uncertain time for your teenager. Mainly because in the relationships and all the togetherness they experience, they are confirmed that they are like the others – which is also called 'normal'. If they are outside that circle, most will turn the blame inward and conclude that they are different from most – or 'not normal' – which can start the downward inner blaming spiral. And shame is powerful. It is tough, but rarely does it sound as bad when said out loud to friends or to you as it does in their heads. Whether or not there is a healthy environment available to grow with friends, it is still possible later in life. Most problems in life can be overcome with togetherness and love. One good friendship where laughter and crying together are possible is worth more than 25 superficial friendships that would fizzle out anyway. Remember that!

The five love languages

I read a book on the five languages of love many years ago, written by Gary Chapman. It was like the piece I was missing in understanding why what I was doing for my partner was not received as intended fell into place. I found that we sometimes misunderstood each other and didn't feel loved and recognised; it could create distance and despair if the other did not recognise our attempt. According to Chapman, the five love languages are:

- **Words of affirmation**: compliments or words of encouragement
- **Acts of service**: setting the table, walking the dog, or doing other small jobs
- **Receiving gifts**: symbols of love, like flowers or chocolates
- **Quality time**: their partner's undivided attention
- **Physical touch**: having sex, holding hands, kissing

A new one has been added – the sixth love language; feeling known. This is when someone truly knows who you are inside and remembers the little details you've told them. However, this love language is up for debate as many believe it is just a combination of all the love languages. For others, it hits the spot as it is the most accurate for them. I love it and feel hugely heard when someone remembers details that I didn't think they had picked up on. That's why I think it should be included, even if it may not be widely accepted.

I later found that everyone in my family had different preferences where they felt loved. Sometimes, several over-lapped, but knowing them was an essential prerequisite for finding closeness and affection with my loved ones. When you feel separated from the people you care about, life can be a lonely place, which is one of the biggest challenges among adolescents today. Knowing your love language can help you communicate more clearly what you need from others, including friends. Or it can help you find ways to connect with the one who you love, using their love lan-guage. I don't find Chapman's definitions black and white, I am sure there are many variations in between, but they are a great inspiration to me. I am aware of how we all feel loved differently, and I strive to understand what love language those close to me have. I have a mixed first place myself: quality time and acts of service – feeling known could also be one of them. My daughters know that, and they consciously set aside time for card games, togetherness and closeness, conversations, walks and cosy dinners with me. It makes me feel warm inside.

Falling in love

Love is probably one of the areas that has gained the most scientific attention over time, and there are groundbreaking studies that include the first functional MRI images (fMRI) of individuals' brains in the context of romantic love. I remember how a good friend in my circle of friends was slowly transformed into my first love when I was a teenager. After a ski trip, I knew I was in love and called him one night and told him how I felt. Luckily for me, it was mutual, and he became my boyfriend. We saw each other often, and when we were not together, I had one of his sweatshirts lying around so I could always smell his scent.

I have seen both my daughters move into the beautiful universe of love and listened to songs about passion, electricity and how 'when you touch me, it's so powerful' from the sidelines. I love when my daughter Julie's boyfriend jogs from the nearby city where he has been partying all night and abruptly wants to run home to her, even though no transport is available. It is dedication and young love beyond all bounds. He is strong, spontaneous and loves her wholeheartedly, whereas Julie embraces him beautifully with her calmness, deep love and drive. It is wonderful and a gift to see your children grow older and experience the intoxication of falling in love, with all its facets, intensity and depth. I am a fan, I must say, because everything becomes possible at once, and unique energy arises.

Brain scans show that considerable activity occurs in some

brain regions when hit by Cupid's arrow. The activity is a result of the chemistry going on. Whether sexual attraction, infatuation, or love, these emotions are born of a complicated interplay of hormones, neurotransmitters and brain areas. A study conducted in 2005 by biological anthropologist Helen Fisher analysed 2,500 brain scans of college students, finding that when shown images of someone special to them, the students' brains became active in dopamine-rich areas, the so-called feel-good neurotransmitter. Two brain areas that showed activity in these fMRI scans were the caudate nuclei associated with reward detection and expectation; the integration of sensory experiences into social behaviour.

When you fall in love, chemicals associated with the reward cycle flood your brain and produce a range of physical and emotional reactions – fast-beating hearts, sweaty palms, flushed cheeks, feelings of passion, and anxiety. The levels of the stress hormone cortisol rise in the initial phase of romantic love, rushing your body to cope with this 'crisis'. When cortisol levels rise, the levels of the neurotransmitter serotonin are depleted. Low levels of serotonin are associated with the obsessions associated with falling in love. Being in love also releases high levels of dopamine, a chemical that 'gets the reward system going' like in gaming. Dopamine activates the reward cycle and helps make love a pleasurable experience, similar to the euphoria associated with cocaine or alcohol use. So it is quite addictive, and no wonder I have felt the electricity in the house increase when my daughters are in love.

Teenagers must go through the phases that life brings

them. Falling in love is one of them, which means many emotions to accommodate and understand. But they will also face sexual experiences, boundaries, and learning how to avoid being infected with a venereal disease or getting pregnant.

When love hurts

I remember when my first love broke up with me. I lay in my bed all day crying, and I thought life would come to a standstill without anyone wanting me to stop crying or move on fast. I sensed nothing but the pain and allowed myself to dive deep into the feeling for hours until I felt empty within. I simply had no more tears in me; I felt calm and thus exhausted. I had given myself the chance to react, and my body seemed peaceful and quiet. I took a few days to recover – walking in a fog – but slowly, I was ready to move on, knowing that the two of us were probably about to break up anyway. Neither my mother nor father tried to intervene but let me calm down and go through this process until I reached out to them again. I am sure my mother must have worn out the carpet pacing in the living room out of concern for me, but she never let me know. I did not try to suppress how I felt, and I was given time to be in my emotions, which I have since taken with me and passed on to my daughters.

One of the finest ways to comfort I experienced on the sidelines was when one daughter had broken up with her boyfriend. Clearly, she was sad afterwards and needed some alone time to settle herself. Her good friend transferred a small amount of money to my daughter's bank account so she could buy an ice cream that could give her some enjoyment in a tough time. I found it such a beautiful gesture. Sometimes you need to know that you are not alone, feeling the care and presence of those close to you without them showing up physically.

Feeling your child's pain and following them closely in their life processes is a gift that brings joy and pain at the same time. It is insanely hard when they are not feeling good. It goes into the bone marrow and torments you. It hurts, and even though you feel like removing all the pain from your teen and sweeping every single stone away from their path, they have to walk that path themselves. Anything else would be a disservice. Your teenager will respond intuitively to the transformation that they sense in you. If you let them see in your eyes that you are worried, they will adopt that. You must never forget that everything helps form the cornerstones of what partner and the kind of love your teen will find in the long run. That pain is also equal to love, which is similar to living and thus a good life lesson. Life will go on. They must be able to get up again themselves.

I had a client whose teenager came home one day, crying, unable to hide that his girlfriend had started to distance herself from him. It was a feeling that created turmoil in him. He felt no longer welcome at her place and was seized by his worst fear because this was the saddest thing that could happen now in his life. After all, he was still very much in love with her. All alarm bells in his mother responded immediately that this was a serious sign of a break-up coming. Her own nervous system took over, as she saw all sorts of frightening scenarios for her, with months of depression and shattered dreams for her son. She couldn't stop herself and pushed so much guilt and so many solutions on him that they ended up in a massive fight.

Yes, you can't always control your feelings; that's how it is. But you must try not to project your adult thoughts, worries and fears of a possible break-up onto your teen in these situations. Nor in other contexts. This mother was well-intended, but her boy regrets to the utmost that he couldn't hide his worries and expressed them to his mother. By chance she was there when he came home from school, and it suddenly was more about her than him.

Therefore, a kindly reminder that you must share your thoughts and adult concerns with your partner and not with your teenager. You must separate your emotions from them; anything else would be unreasonable to put on the shoulders of your growing adolescent. They have much to deal with themselves and, first and foremost, need a shoulder to cry on, not a lesson in what has been done wrong. Give them the powerful gift of attention, if they ask for it. They will need you to be their supporter in painful processes. Let them know that they are not alone and that you are available if they need to talk. The roads lead to the same thing, one way or another, and it is impossible to go through life and not experience broken hearts a few times. Cherish the beauty of having been so privileged to feel the depth and intensity of love and togetherness. Therein lies the gift, and without it, its opposite would not exist.

CHAPTER 7

Uniqueness

WHO AM I?

'Finding yourself' is perhaps a lifelong process, as new insights can constantly emerge that slightly shift your perceptions of who you are. However, for your teenager, experiencing themselves as an independent individual and feeling comfortable with their own identity becomes paramount at the end of adolescence. Only when they have freed themselves sufficiently from their environment can they become an independent 'identity', according to developmental psychologist Erik H. Erikson.

> 'Identity' originates from a Latin word (*identitas*), meaning oneness, equality. The root of the word is *idem*, which means 'same'. Identity means an awareness of who you are, where you belong, or the awareness of belonging to a particular culture or a particular social group.

To have an identity means to be true to yourself, in different situations, at different times and with different people. You are the same today as you were yesterday and you know who you want to be tomorrow. You have coherence and continuity in your individual life story, your biography. This self-perception contains everything you discern to be you: appearance, age, gender, talent, social status, unique character traits like sensitive, clumsy, clever, adventurous, funny and so on, plus the experiences and reflections from your life that all together give you the understanding that this is who I am. Your story about yourself is thus linked to your identity.

Through my conversations with teens in my practice and with my children's friends, I have noticed that they have a pretty casual relationship with diagnoses today and talk openly and honestly about mental well-being. I find this interesting because having a therapist signals that you are taking care of your mental health. Our generation has helped us recognise the need for this. Still, going from there to using diagnoses like anxiety, ADHD, autism, or schizotypy to define who they are as the most natural thing, I am genuinely curious about as a societal phenomenon. I think we are made to find ways to survive if life is complicated and insurmountable, so perhaps the younger generation has unknowingly found a legitimate way to get a break in a demanding and achievement-driven world. If they have a diagnosis, it is acceptable and expected not to have to live up to the many demands of being unique in the world open to them.

Today, when we let our children know that they are unique and amazing as they are and that the world is open to them, it can feel like there are many demands they have to meet. Of course, our intentions are good, but the flip side is that no one can live up to such a high standard in the long run, where uniqueness and perfection are the parameters that define who they are. As a result, many may find they don't measure up – they're not good enough, or not happy enough, or they're ungrateful.

It is a vulnerable state to be a teenager and to have to tinker with identifying with different adult role models (you or significant others), while at the same time distancing yourself from what you have always leant on. They cannot find out who they are without being in an emotionally close relationship with you. At the same time there is enormous societal pressure on your teen today. They encounter it in every aspect of their life – at home, at school, at leisure activities, and, of course, via social media. There is undeniably a lot to live up to and many choices that can cause anxiety and inferiority complexes because nothing is good enough or like the 'others'. Being their best supporters, this is a time that requires your patience and understanding.

All bodies are beautiful

Today, body image is utterly different than in, for example the 1980s, when I was an insecure teenager.

I have an untroubled relationship with my body. I never speak ill of it. I can casually walk naked to the bathroom and back because it is essential to show my daughters that their bodies and nudity are not wrong or sexualising. As a child growing up in Denmark in the 1970s, nudity was also quite common. I remember countless summers when my parents and their friends lay in the dunes by the North Sea, talking and laughing while soaking up the sun and enjoying the heat of summer – naked. We children collected seaweed or covered our naked bodies with sand, threw ourselves into the waves of the sea, and only ran back to the adults if we were going to have some snacks and something to drink. It was all perfectly natural.

Times have changed, and today many may consider such a Danish way of being natural around nudity as wrong or detrimental, which I strongly disagree with. It is more impor-tant than ever to teach your children that their bodies are their temples. They are beautiful as they are, and that under expensive clothes and filters, there is a body of skin and bones with a beating heart. That can never be something wrong.

Via social media, there is a tendency now to focus on perfect bodies, like Barbie figures. All adolescents live in the shadow of this culture of perfection today, where many of their stars risk being extinguished. No one should live in the belief that the body with which they were created is wrong or ugly. Both those who identify as girls and boys tell me, when I meet them in my counselling, that they have complexes about their appearance. They know that height and muscles are important for boys, while the buttocks, lips and breasts are for girls. An attempt is made to live up to a particular ideal, which generates uncertainty and low self-esteem when it is not achieved. Therefore, plastic surgery has increased explo-sively, and also among teenagers. Both teenagers and adults are very concerned about 'how they look'. According to the

American Society of Plastic and Reconstructive Surgeons, by 2020 nearly 230,000 cosmetic surgeries and about 140,000 non-invasive cosmetic procedures were performed on teens aged 13–19. Although there are no precise figures on how many teens have cosmetic procedures in Denmark, we know the numbers are rising rapidly. Teens everywhere are much more exposed to social media and are becoming increasingly critical of their percived flaws like a double chin, wrinkles, thick thighs or big noses.

According to Danish plastic surgeons, patients no longer take pictures of celebrities to consultations for reference but digitally enhanced pictures of themselves. They want sharp cheekbones, large lips, white teeth, and narrower noses. In the wake of all the new image-editing options and apps, a new type of body disorder has emerged, which researchers call 'Snapchat dysmorphia', related to Body Dysmorphic Syndrome (BDS). BDS refers to a mental disorder in which you have a very distorted perception of your own body. The perceived problem takes up too much mental space. The patient is overfocused, giving too much attention to the body image and not just what most people experience every now and then as a 'bad day'. They create filters in the pictures, for example, the slightly cartoon-like faces you can make on Snapchat, where the eyes are made a little bigger and the chin smaller so that you actually look like a mouse or Bambi.

Teens (like adults) seek plastic surgery to improve their appearance or to increase self-esteem. Some of the most common types of plastic surgery that teens choose include 'nose jobs', and correction of protruding ears, oversized breasts, asymmetrical breasts, and scarring caused by acne or injuries. But breast augmentation surgeries for teens 17 years or younger constitute 12.2 per cent of such procedures world-wide, even though breasts can grow until you are 21 years old.

One of the reasons given by many is that young people can be brutal, whether intentionally or not. They are some-times quick to judge and can comment as a friend passes by, 'Geez, did you see his nose?' Or 'Look at her, she's flat as a board' – without thinking about the real hurt it can cause. Unfortunately, it can have severe consequences for the sus-ceptible teenager who hears it, which of course is not the intention. For most, such comments are a way of making them feel less dissatisfied with themselves, which they haven't found any other way to cope with yet. But it may explain why so many teenagers change their looks. Maybe my daughters will also change their appearances one day. Many report that their self-image and self-confidence improve when their perceived physical shortcomings are corrected. I will, then, support them, if it is not a decision made in a hurry. Do I have another choice? No, so that is why I'll always have their back, even if it is not necessarily something I advocate.

While your teenagers are still open to guidance, and you want to teach them about body differences, I can highly rec-ommend visiting a public swimming pool or sauna with your kids as much as possible. Places where there is a culture of safe and healthy nudity. If you visit a Danish swimming pool, everyone showers naked (divided by gender, of course) before they are allowed to swim in the water. If you visit a sauna, which is very popular, everyone sits naked together – both men and women. However, some choose to sit with a small towel over their lower parts while others don't. Winter bathing nude in the sea (and year round) has become extremely popular during the pandemic for both adolescents and adults, so if you visit Denmark, you will find that we are no strangers to each other on this point. Danish teenagers are just as influenced by the culture of perfection as teenagers elsewhere, but they can come across all body shapes if they want. If they want to they can experience the differences central to achieving a natural and accepting relationship with their body. After all, no one really is either Barbie or Ken.

Being around others of *all* ages taking showers before going to the swimming pool, in the dressing room after sports, freezing in sub-zero temperatures after a dive in the sea, or sweating in saunas, nudity can feel incredibly liberating when done naturally in the proper setting. I hope that nudity in itself can be kept separate from anything sexualising or 'naughty'. As long as a norm or culture defines the context and therefore normalises its purpose, children and teens shouldn't be kept away from it. This transition period of your teens' lives is about them having to accept just who they are – not looking like their idols or the filtered images on social media, but loving themselves fully and truly.

Pimples

Pimples, pubic hair and sweat odour are a part of everyday life for all teenagers. I was no exception. I remember the first pimple I got on my chin when I was around 12 or 13 years old. It was an affirmation that I had officially become a teenager. But at the same time, it was distorting the view I had of myself, and I wanted it to go away. I had recently been introduced to an innovative little plastic tool which, with a light grip, could suck the sting out of a foot if someone had been stung by a bee. It was super smart because the problem was fixed in less than a minute, and life could go on again without any pain. Here my first little inflamed pimple made me decide to do something about it. So I picked up that sucking device for bee stings, put it over the pimple, and pulled all I could. I felt proud and technologically superior to what industry could come up with. I knew that my impressive invention would be something all teens would thank me for when they saw the change it easily made to me. After finishing my removal, I went to the mirror. To my shock, the pimple was completely intact. Unwittingly, I had given myself a colossal suction mark. Which made everything worse and was hard to hide and explain to my friends. My bubbling self-confidence instantly vanished, and I had to accept both the good and the bad of being a teenager.

Almost all teens get acne. It happens when an oily substance called sebum clogs the pores. Pimples usually appear on the face, neck, back, chest and shoulders. Acne is not a severe health problem, although acute acne can cause lasting scars and intense insecurity. No one fully understands how acne affects self-esteem if they haven't had it. Even mild outbreaks can make you feel insecure and unattractive. The lack of self-confidence can make it difficult to face others, participate in social life, and interact with the opposite sex.

Teenagers are well aware that their pimples are the first thing others see; this is how they experience it. In a culture characterised by perfection I understand how it can feel hard to believe otherwise. As mentioned before, the world can be harsh among teenagers. Being exposed and humiliated due to pimply skin can cost many extinguished stars. It is a huge problem for those who go through their teens with this challenge. It does not always help to say 'no one notices it' because they know it's not true. The face is the first thing you look at, and here you get the first impression of the person you meet, so don't be tempted to ignore it for your teenager. In order to meet them in their pain, as well as to provide a subtle sense of hope, I would say that they are beautiful and that it is not that bad.

There is way too much attention paid to appearance today, so it helps to focus on something else. As a parent, you can help with that. First of all, show by your actions more important things to focus on than their appearance. Show your true side in front of your teen; don't always wear make-up and remember to talk positively about yourself. If you have struggled with acne, you can tell them about what it did to your self-esteem. It is OK to say that it made you sad because your teenager can reflect on that. You can also tell anecdotes that created embarrassment for you, maybe laugh a bit when looking back to make the situation lighter, but at the same time, describe how you got through this period of your life.

Remember that your teenager looks upon you as being strong and capable. You're proof that it's possible to get through it and have a wonderful life today.

Recognising that it is a difficult and distressing time is an important first step. But cultivating their self-esteem by strengthening their empathetic abilities and good values also has enormous significance. Focus on challenging them mentally as well as physically and let them become good at something they love. It gives self-esteem and an inner glow that makes them radiate confidence. It is not a cliché that it is what's inside that counts.

If you focus not only on the outside but also the inside, your teen will be better able to accept their pimples. I have always tried to focus on teaching my girls that beauty comes from within. If you are not beautiful on the inside, then you'll never be truly beautiful. Radiance means everything and although pimples are embarrassing and trigger extreme insecurity, it is essential to focus on what strengthens self-esteem. Pimples will eventually go away. You want your teen to come out of this ready to conquer the world.

Periods

Do you call your period 'the curse', 'that time of the month', 'Aunt Flo', or 'Code Red'? If so, you are not alone. A dear child has many names, as the saying goes. But suppose you could exchange those code words for something more positive. In that case, your teenager would grow used to hearing

about menstruation as a normal and natural biological function that will follow them for many years.

When I got my first period, my mother applauded it by
congratulating me. For it was a beautiful event that meant I
was on my way into the adult world, that I was fertile. I could
now embrace the femininity that I had longed for even though
I was terrified and insecure and didn't really know how to
embrace the new very inevitable side of me. I applauded my
daughters in the same way, and if it happened in school while
I was a teacher, the students were celebrated the same way.
I like to look at menstruation as a gift, something life-giving
women are fortunate to carry, which enables the human race
to survive.

I sometimes hear, though, how this beautiful gift is
degraded and referred to as 'disgusting', 'dirty', 'unclean', or
something one should be 'kept away from'. I crumble inside
and have a difficult time understanding where this stigma
comes from. And if that isn't enough, menstruation is also
often spoken of condescendingly to explain why a person
has PMS or is behaving in a sensitive, explicit, or hostile
manner. How a beautiful, natural and life-giving word can
elicit so much negativity is beyond me. Looking back, some
religions have historically had rules discriminating against
menstruating women. Sex was forbidden during menstruation and menstruating women would be refered to as 'one
who is excluded' or 'expelled'. Thankfully this was long ago
and times have changed. But maybe not enough. I believe
that we are experiencing a slow and long-awaited stigma shift.
Menstruation is an essential part of life. It's normal, natural

and occurs regularly for about 40 years, for those who have frequent menses. We would not be here if it were not so.

I have always had a relaxed way of approaching menstruation. I have never suffered from severe pain during ovulation, or heavy bleeding. I have had an entirely natural awareness of my body's needs in all aspects and have always known intuitively when it needed some care due to hormones or stress. Sometimes I lay on the couch and just allowed myself to do nothing. Other times I jogged, ate chocolate (a little too much), watched a sitcom, or had a massage. Whatever made me feel OK I allowed to happen, and that worked for me. It might not work for you, but if you pay attention to your body's signals and are sensitive to its workings, I believe that you are doing some important care for yourself.

In recent years our culture has seen a rise in menstrual activism that aims to put the stigma of periods in the past. This is also called menstrual anarchy or menarchy, which is positive. Céline Brassart Olsen, a lawyer and researcher in menstrual health, offers guidance to mothers and daughters so they can befriend their menstrual cycle and see it as a blessing rather than a curse. She shared this:

Most girls are handed a pack of sanitary pads when they have their first period, and told that they can get pregnant now. Our culture offers little reverence for this rite of passage into womanhood. There is however, a completely different way to look at our menstrual cycle. Ancient cultures recognized menstruation as a time of heightened awareness, sensitivity and wisdom for women, which required them to slow down. Organising a small ritual, such as sharing a handwritten letter with your daughter, gifting her a small piece of jewellery, or having a small ceremony can be a powerful way to honour menarche. Inviting her to slow down and to tune into her inner world when her period starts to appear regularly can also help her grow comfortable with this potent time of the month.

These are powerful practices, because when we make something sacred, it stops being shameful.

Breaking voices

In the same way that menstruation can be perceived as taboo and shamful in many places, there are also phases in a boy's life that are subject to humiliation, albeit to a lesser degree. When boys reach puberty, the larynx begins to grow and becomes visible at the front of the throat. This is what is called the Adam's apple. As the larynx grows, the voice transitions and deepens, which can happen more or less overnight. Teenage boys will often find that their voice 'breaks' or 'cracks' when they speak. This is a phase that many boys fear and at the same time look forward to. It is exciting to become more mature, but it's also embarrassing to be the focus of attention when your voice is squeaking and cracking and sounding goofy.

As a teacher in many different classes, I have experienced all forms and degrees of voice breaks. Since I do not have sons myself, I have not experienced it in my private life. Still, I have always been conscious of letting the boys who went through this know that they were completely normal. No laughter, no humiliation, but eye contact and certainty that everything was as it should be, and that their voice would soon be under their control again.

How long their voice is in transition differs from boy to boy. Because it is such a sensitive time, we as parents have a great responsibility to inform our sons what is happening to them and why. Being in a state of uncertainty creates a lot of misconceptions and fosters low self-esteem.

I meet teenage boys in my consultations who do not talk to their parents or friends about their body's development and sexuality. I will return to the subject of sexuality a little later, but they are confused and do not understand the changes they are experiencing. 'Why is it that my voice is cracking?' 'Why am I not growing taller like my friends?' 'Why can I not control my erection?' 'Why do I feel embarrassed and ashamed?' 'Why do I have wet dreams?' Although some of the teenage boys I meet have a good relationship with one or both of their parents, many overlook their sons' need to have deep, informative conversations about what is happening during this period of their life.

One could get the impression that boys are being ignored in this area simply because they are boys. In part, I think it is because conversations about more intimate topics are often difficult for many adults. It simply feels embarrassing and awkward for even the best-prepared parent. I also think it has to do with the fact that many parents simply do not feel the need is there. Their teenage boys hide more of their feelings, isolate themselves in their room with computer games, or are out of the house doing physical activities. On the whole they also speak with fewer words than girls do. So it's easy to assume that they do not have the same need for dialogue that it is instantly obvious girls do. I believe this to be a misconception. Gaining most of their sexual knowledge from watching porn online or from friends who are most likely exaggerating can cause misunderstandings in their perception of themselves, their boundaries and expectations. Teenage boys also benefit significantly from having a place where all kinds of questions and insecurities can be dealt with in a safe environment and they can learn to express feelings and needs in the same way as girls. Actually, I would prefer to erase everything that has to do with gender stigmas and just focus on creating a safe place where all teenagers can come to us with their insecurities without being ashamed or feeling foolish, irrespective of wet dreams or blood on the sheet.

In my home, it has always been natural for my girls to come to me with their very intimate questions. Nevertheless they prefer to go to their father with some things. Similarly, I know of fathers to teenage boys who will invite their sons into a safe private space. It could be taking a walk together or going for a ride in the car, just the two of them. Times like that can be a golden opportunity for teenagers to piece together some of the things that are puzzling them. This is not to say that a mother–son or a father–daughter conversation can't be optimal for you. You just have to feel it yourself and go for what you think is best for your teenager. Creating a safe space to acquire new concepts and a deeper understanding of the many new feelings and changes is basically the essence of what can make a big difference. Being able to mirror oneself in the thoughts of a more experienced adult is essential for the feeling of being understood. Voice breaks, mood swings, sweat odour and body hair need to be articulated and normalised.

Inclusion

Today, it doesn't matter if you define yourself as a boy or a girl. Not everyone is homosexual or heterosexual. So, how do you as a parent avoid putting your teenager in a box like 'a typical girl' or 'a typical boy' and instead support them in being just themselves? The other day I observed two children meeting each other for the first time. One asked the other, 'Are you a boy?' To which the other replied, 'No.' 'Are you a girl then?' 'No, I am just a person.' The one who asked just accepted it, and they started playing. I found this quite inspiring. I have experienced parents who were embarrassed that their boy loved wearing pink dresses as a child and were afraid of what it could mean for their future. I can understand that. As parents, you want your children to go through life with the fewest bumps and challenges possible, and if you do not fit right into the usual norms, there is a greater risk that the road will be full of potholes.

First, it is good to be able to distinguish between gender and sexuality. These two things are often confused, although there is a pervasive distinction: here is a girl – her gender. She is attracted to boys, what you call heterosexual – that is her sexuality. When your baby is born, the midwife looks at the visible genitals to determine if your baby is a boy or a girl. It is unproblematic for the vast majority of people because the gender on the birth certificate corresponds to the gender the person feels like. This is what is also called being cis-gendered. Cis means 'to be on the same page'. So you are a cisgender when you are on the same page as the gender you were born with. But others grow up without feeling comfortable with their gender. LGBTQ+ people see gender as three things that can point in different directions: how the body is created, biologically (called sex). The gender you perceive yourself to be (called gender). And then the gender expression itself, for example, what clothes you wear. This category strongly depends on the culture you live in.

Suppose you want to talk to your teenager about gender and sexuality. In that case, I suggest that you be a role model for diversity or search for information online. It is not wrong to like pink dresses when you are a girl and to play with action figures when you are a boy. But it is OK to challenge those gender stereotypes about whether boys can wear pink and girls can play with action figures. The less prejudiced you are, the more inclusive and included you make your child feel – and later on your teen.

Some mistakenly think that they can stimulate their teen's feminine or masculine sides if they only play with gender-specific toys. It might be insecurity within the parent that can force them to encourage their boys to play soccer to make them 'real men' or buy pink dresses for their girls who prefer to climb trees, if they sense they are about to go in another direction. That's very stereotypically put, but the difficulties of embracing children and teens fully are often revealed because you have some biased notions about how your teenagers should fit into the expected boxes of normality – and therein which stars should be extinguished or not. This is quite common since what you don't know much about feels scary. Who wants their teen to stand out as being different? Not many. Whatever your teen feels like, it can't be suppressed. So instead of having to hide sides of themselves and turn off significant stars, you could meet them where they are, with understanding curiosity, and be a part of changing 'normal' a bit.

The language you use is extremely powerful and defining. What were you called as a child? Maybe some of those labels are stuck to your identity today and have cost extinguished stars. As already mentioned, I was called demanding, and it's not very nice to cause others distress so of course I learnt to adapt and make myself useful. How do you talk about other people in front of your teen? Do you respect their wishes if they want to be called something specific? Do you label typical characteristics those of girls and boys, respectively? Do you use words like 'girl' or 'boy'? How do you react when you walk the streets with your teen and meet a transgender person? Do you smile? Or maybe you come up with a half-funny comment? I am not sure we can always react perfectly and avoid crossing others' boundaries. Still, we can make an effort to pay attention to whether what we say is coloured by our own values and norms or whether we express openness and inclusion.

Practise asking curious questions of your teenager and acknowledge with interest what they see – not as the expert who has answers to all questions. Always consider your teen's boundaries and be careful about asking questions that go too close to your teen's sexuality or gender. Once you have crossed a boundary, it can be difficult to regain their confidence. Instead, be patient and accept that they don't want to share everything with you. Instead, consider yourself as their kind facilitator. The emotional connection is important to keep in mind when talking to your teen. Be empathetic and keep an eye on how long and how much your teen wants to talk to you about these things.

Sexuality

The first time I experienced a certain tingling in my stomach was as an 11-year-old. I was on holiday with my father, sister and cousin, bicycling across the country. At one place we stayed, we got into a conversation with a sweet boy of the same age. He looked at me with warmth and a special kind of interest that I had not experienced before, and I felt a connection between us that was very new to me. I buried it quickly as I was a little embarrassed about what happened within me, but it was stored in my mind for ever.

Sexuality is a necessary and inherent part of human development and well-being and a central aspect of teenagers' identity formation. The World Health Organisation's broad definition of sexuality can help us understand the diversity of sub-elements at stake that impact teenagers' sexual development:

> Sexuality is an integral part of every person's personality. It is a basic need and an aspect of being human that is inseparable from other aspects of life. Sexuality is not synonymous with intercourse. It is not about whether we have an orgasm or not, and finally, it is not the sum of our erotic lives. This may be part of our sexuality, but it need not be. Sexuality is so much more. That is what drives us to seek love, warmth, and intimacy. It is expressed in the way we feel, move, touch, and are touched. It is as much this to be sensual as to be sexual.
>
> Sexuality affects our thoughts, feelings, actions, and interactions, thereby our mental and physical health. And since health is a fundamental human right, sexual health must also be a basic human right.

This describes sexuality as the physical and mental energy that makes us seek love, warmth and intimacy, expressed in how we feel, move, touch and are touched. Therefore, sex, passion and lust are not dirty or wrong but fantastic and enriching.

I am a private person, but I still think it is important to talk about sexuality with the greatest naturalness in the world. In general terms, in the same way I speak to my children and clients about death, grief, fear and happiness, I talk with my daughters about sexuality. Lust and the desire to explore this sexual world do not disappear for your teens simply because you don't talk about it.

Therefore, the foundations of knowledge and information laid at home equip them to better understand their
own thoughts and feelings, desires and boundaries. Not
necessarily with face-to-face conversation in which the bees
and flowers unfold, but, as I always highlight, much of this
foundation work takes place in the years of childhood – how
positively you talk about your body, how much you have
taught them to respect a 'no', how you respond to questions
while they arise and before your teenager finds them embarrassing. Once your teen has started having sexual fantasies, it
usually becomes more awkward to talk about it with you. You
can let them know that they can always come to you if they
have questions, make yourself available and speak positively
about others. At the same time, you can watch reality shows
with them, for example, to reflect on what they are being
exposed to. I have always told my girls that what they see on
TV is not the norm but performed by someone who may be
exaggerating a little – or a lot. If I say something now, my
girls promptly answer me, 'Yes, yes, Mum, we know this is
not necessarily standard.' Personally, I may be a little worried about hearing young people in reality series exaggerate
sex in a way that sounds like it is something mechanical
that is only there to quickly satisfy a need. And when they
simultaneously refer to anal sex and 1,000 positions as the
new variety, I fear that the many young people who follow
and look up to these reality stars think that this is the norm
and, therefore, what they can be expected to engage in. No
wonder so many fear this phase as performance anxiety must
be so high assuming that everything seen is normal. Maybe

I am a bit old school – if what teens do feels OK with them, I'm fine too. But, there is something limitless about this, and it frightens me.

Porn

In the same way that five love languages are defined by Gary Chapman, there are also five sex languages defined by Jaiya, an award-winning sexologist and creator of Ignite Your Passion. She is committed to helping people create deep love and hot, juicy passion. According to her, the five sex languages are:

- **Energetic**, preoccupied with tantra and/or yoga, and focused on feeling their bodies' energy
- **The sensual** is romantic and loves long massages with hot oils, evocative, quiet music and extended foreplay before sex
- Then there is **the sexual** who likes to drop the foreplay and go straight to the fun. Penetration is fun, and quickies are naughty hot sex
- Next, there is **the kinky**, who is both creative and curious and loves adventure. It can be sex in new places, like in nature with long playful sessions
- Last, but not least there is **the shapeshifter**, who switches between all the sex languages. They may be in all the different spectrums but still have a core in their sexuality

As with the love languages that have helped me better give my daughters the love they understand, the five sex languages may also provide inspiration in helping to understand the differences between desires so that the boundaries of what they like can be better defined and normalised. As well as gaining awareness that sex and desires can look different, all depending on who you are.

It is problematic that many young people educate themselves in sex through porn. It creates some distorted images of what they need to go out and perform. Porn is a subject that causes many misunderstandings between teenagers entering this new field of sex as it has nothing to do with reality. Porn is performance sex that affects the brain and the way your teen relates to people. Porn is not necessarily bad, and I do not want to speak for or against it, but one thing is for sure: it is very different from real sex – or what is done in the bedroom. There is no deep intimacy, no real passion, and no groping interest in the body and its erogenous zones in a shared bubble of authentic desire.

Teenagers just do not know this! They do not know that what they watch is a performance with actors without an emotional connection, a performance that considers camera angles and how the actors can sit, lie or stand, with simulated sounds, so it works best for the viewer, regardless of whether it has anything to do with reality. Teenagers are convinced that is what they are going to do. It picks up on their body insecurity as they need to emulate what they see in porn, both the physical appearance and the action. Boys learn that they need a giant penis with a constant hard erection to please their chosen ones. They also learn that the girl is always aroused and gets orgasms in one go. No one tells them about anatomy and right angles. Nor does anyone tell them that the scenes where the man cannot get an erection are edited out. Porn teaches them that the guy is always hard and ready, while the girl is willing, aroused and open.

I read a lot about how porn today destroys young people's perceptions of sex and intimacy – and that not everyone can distinguish between real and staged intercourse, with women who have had plastic surgery and no longer appear natural as they were created, but instead as Lolita figures that no one can (or should) live up to. It can set unreasonable pressure for how girls should look and how they should act in bed. Similarly, I am aware of young men who cannot get an erection when lying with their teenage love because she does not have a body like the women they have masturbated to in porn. Not to mention because of doubt and nervousness.

Performance anxiety about sex is one of the most common problems for many young people with sexual difficulties. Today, it is not rare for relationships to occur virtually, where teens can easily present themselves favourably. One of the consequences is that authentic relationships, where they must be close to each other physically, become more complicated. There is something distorted about the development that is going on right now. That is why I am including it in this book, as the use of potency drugs has apparently increased for teenage boys quite dramatically.

According to the Danish Health and Medicines Authority, the number of young people between 18 and 24 who have bought prescription potency drugs has increased from just over 150 people in 1999 to approximately 1,000 in 2019. Also, in the age group between 25 and 44, there is a marked increase. In 1999, about 3,000 people bought prescription potency drugs, while that number twenty years later had risen to almost 14,000. Potency drugs can cause problems with blood pressure and headaches if not taken with care. Therefore, it is an area where I think you can do more for your teen so that they take better care of themselves, lower their expectations, and learn to distinguish between fantasy and reality. Since a teenager's brain does not know this by itself, there is a danger that there will be a mismatch between fantasy and reality in the long run in this area. Here you can teach them some good tools to create a safe space between them and the one they are intimate with, where it is OK to be nervous and insecure. And where it is OK if it does not go well initially, because there is no rush. Dialogue, contact and presence are the way forward.

In most countries, there will be sex education in schools, where specific topics are touched upon in collaboration with the other students in the class. This can feel awkward and uncomfortable for some and will not necessarily lead to the intended result. Therefore, your position as a parent is to adapt how you react and what you say to precisely the needs and questions relevant to your teenager. You can help them put their own thoughts and experiences into words and let them know that it is perfectly OK – and in fact essential – to learn a language for this completely normal part of their development.

The world needs differences, nuances and greater tolerance for diversity. We are currently witnessing a Generation Z that is exceptionally open, turning many norms upside down. It may be hard to understand it all, but we too will have to accept it with openness and curiosity. We achieve nothing out of making their investigations and breaches of norms wrong. Do not let the differences separate us, but instead aim to meet others with tolerance and an open mind. The least we can do is try and make an effort to never compromise the relationship.

Witnessing the change that our teenager has to go through is a beautiful and delicate gift we must cherish. They who were once considered a child are now moving on to having a different status, which they will bring into their adult lives forever. How priceless!

CHAPTER 8

No Ultimatums

EMBRACE THEM WHILE RAGING

I have counselled parents from many cultures and countries who believed they should show their authority by raising their voice and dictating that rules and ultimatums should be obeyed. They weren't able to listen or compromise, even though they may have intended to, and they felt they were losing respect when their teen did not submit to them. Something in them wanted to change even though they did not know how, as they were stuck in a challenging situation that they didn't understand. It was creating distance in their relationships with their adolescent so they tried to soften their approach, looking for the bigger perspective. Good intentions that I think every parent can understand.

In Denmark, most parents won't use their 'power' in such a way, because we strive for a more level parenting system as opposed to a hierarchy of dominance. Sure, there are all kinds of approaches here. Nevertheless, most Danes engage their teenagers in a more democratic and less authoritarian style. Obedience isn't the main thing, but reciprocity and mutual respect are the focus when dealing with difficulties. When searching for a solution to a problem with our teen it's important not to let the problem overshadow everything else.

Bear in mind what works well and what you appreciate, for they might well point in the direction of a solution without using ultimatums. Acknowledging that we do not always have all the answers, we try to find a way that is conducive to respect and acceptance. Parenting is not something we just do, but something we make an effort to learn by continuously acquiring new coping strategies and knowledge.

Ultimatum is a term used to describe the final requirements of a negotiation. It is inevitable and irreversible in nature.

I do not believe in ultimatums, and I am not an authoritarian parent. I have never used ultimatums, and I have never spanked my kids. I am not faultless at all, but it is simply not in my genetic code. I do not think that getting mad and yelling at my teens does any good. For me, it is important to have give-and-take conversations with them where I explain my reasoning. I believe they learn to think critically and rationally that way. This is imperative, mainly because of the level of information today on social media – full of pitfalls to avoid and opportunities to seize. I encourage independence and autonomy. I practise discussion to explain boundaries, and I see myself as a warm, caring, responsive mother. I put all my vigour into creating a secure attachment that will help them become resilient and better at recovering from setbacks when they happen. I am positive that it will leave them with high self-esteem and confidence enough to make a difference. I love it when they express their opinion and participate in decisions. They have an idea of what to prepare for dinner, how to stand up for their beliefs, what to do after college, and what they love and appreciate when spending time with their friends. I know my children respect me and see me as a powerful woman, and they behave well and do not act in unhealthy ways – at least not very often. Also, they do not doubt that when I say no, I mean it.

Even when I was a teacher, I never raised my voice. When I spoke calmly and respectfully to my students, they responded in kind. Of course, I could be determined and straightforward, but it was achievable without raising my voice. My students were also never in doubt about what I meant. When I stopped being a teacher, they told me that I was strict and demanded much from them, but that I was loving, caring, and their 'school mother'. This is my way of being in the world. It is not necessarily right for others, nor is it true that a good upbringing exists only without ultimatums. Teenagers are all different, and they press our panic buttons differently, which we all try to handle in the best way we can. When things are turbulent there is wisdom to be had and strength to be obtained by recognising what is going on within; why is this happening? Where does this reaction come from? Always remember that if you listen to yourselves, then you know what is best for your teenager even though you might not always have all the answers.

The United Nations Convention on the Rights of the Child is an important agreement by countries who have promised to protect children's rights. The Convention explains who children are, all their rights, and the responsibilities of governments. All the rights are connected, they are all equally important and cannot be taken away from children. A summary of the text of the Convention can be found on the Unicef website at https://www.unicef.org.uk/what-we-do/un-convention-child-rights/

Ultimatums

An ultimatum is a one-way communication tool and a hurtful way to use your power when you feel angry or frustrated and cannot find other strategies to turn to. An ultimatum is a term attributed to the last demands of a negotiation. It is binding and irreversible in nature. When I use the term in parenting, it seems to me to be something impossible to navigate. How can you say, 'Go to your room and do not come out until you have learnt a lesson'? When do you know that a lesson has been learnt, and how do you follow up on it? Rarely does anyone follow up on ultimatums; the only thing you achieve is to leave your teen alone until they come out of the room and say, 'Sorry.' You nod and respond, 'Have you learnt your lesson?' Your teen will nod back, and you may or may not check or even notice if whatever provoked the ultimatum happens again in the future. The only underlying thing you communicate is that love is conditional; you love them when they are 'good' but not when they are 'bad'.

Ultimatums are doomed to fail because they inherently exclude any new learning by explanation or discussion; they are star extinguishers. They make you seem unreliable. There is nothing wrong with setting some clear rules and living by the values you have chosen. But there is a problem if you use an ultimatum as a way to 'punish' your teenager for behaviour you do not find appropriate. Teenagers who have been severely reprimanded, subjected to irrational ultimatums, and have not been met on an emotional level seem to have a little more difficulty dealing with problems later in life, like the example in the chapter on Reframing on page 44. Emotional neglect can leave your teenager uncertain over making decisions. They quickly lose faith in their own abilities. They feel insecure and worried. They have trouble dealing with stress and hardships and perhaps make poor choices that negatively affect the rest of their lives. Study after study shows that ultimatums only promote fear, distance, loneliness and many conflicts, which no one wants for their teen.

That said, situations can arise where there is no other resort than to come up with an ultimatum. Of course, I have knowledge of parents, both professionally and privately, who have experienced their teens acting entirely irresponsibly and dangerously. A young boy stole his father's car, drove too fast and ended up having an accident where he totalled the vehicle. Luckily no one was hurt. Police brought the boy home to the dad, who was asked whether he would report his own boy for stealing the vehicle. Another boy brought his moped inside his house one day, where he disassembled it to repair it. And there have been parents who have had their home wreaked when their teenager has had a party without their knowledge and it has been gatecrashed by uninvited strangers. Some parents are also confronted by teenagers who take drugs or end up in fights.

There are times when you can try to impart all your values and best wishes, but nothing you do reaches your teen's sense. This is also a truth, where it may seem pointless to talk your teen to reason. The frontal lobes are not ready to receive and translate the information yet, so you won't get the response or change in behaviour you hope for.

A wonderful and savvy boy I had in my consultation felt already, at the age of 14, that he did not fit into his family any more. He felt alienated and could no longer identify with the values and norms of his upbringing. He didn't feel seen or recognised for who he was – maybe he never had, but now he had the strength to act on that feeling – and he rebelled against everything that he could, all the time. His parents didn't understand his motives for confronting them, and he was never questioned. For three and a half years, they faced each other down daily. It got more and more destructive between them, only to end up in a cold-hearted and unloving relationship. The ultimatum came, and he was asked to move away from home. No one could stand the negative and draining energy any more. The boy had extinguished many stars, and his parents were exhausted and frustrated.

Sometime after he moved away, their physical and mental distance did make reconciliation possible. They could suddenly find some new and suitable grounds to meet on, which became their starting point for rebuilding all that had broken between them. So, even though many of you are against ultimatums, it can end up being a solution if everything goes awry.

Even for those who want to avoid ending up there, an authoritative approach is not about *not* setting boundaries. On the contrary, setting boundaries is necessary and it must not be compared to giving ultimatums. Setting boundaries can be done by speaking out about what you accept and do not accept. 'When you do this, it frightens me to death. It is simply not OK.' 'Fighting scares me, and I am afraid you'll be stabbed, kicked in the head, and end up brain-damaged or shot. Tell me why you end up in such situations; I want to understand.' 'It's not appropriate to take your moped inside; you mustn't do that again. It belongs outside where you can repair it. OK?' 'When you party without permission, you break the trust I have in you. I trust you, and trust is what makes our family united and special. How can we get back to that?' 'When you confront us and challenge our way of living, what is it that we're not seeing in you?'

When you interact with your teen, it is about communicating your values through your behaviour. It is the ability to see beneath the surface. Knowing your values makes it easier to set boundaries and talk about what you like and dislike as individuals and as a family (much more about this can be found in my online course), especially when there are conflicts which most often arise when there is a mismatch between your expectations of your teen and the teen's perception of what is expected of them. These expectations are rarely adjusted, resulting in conflict or disagreements.

No teenager wants confrontations and will stop co-operating willingly when shouted at or threatened with ultimatums. Instead, their nervous system closes down – a star goes out – and they stop coming to you if they need support or guidance. This is counter to what was initially your intention. To avoid this, you must redirect your attitude instead of using ultimatums to enforce your wishes.

Being an authoritative parent

Unfortunately, many of us misunderstand what an authoritative approach is, as opposed to an authoritarian one. Some think authoritative parents do not have rules, are weak, do not have any authority, or are passive. But these assumptions are incorrect. Unlike an authoritarian parent, who may seem colder and less responsive, authoritative parents respond to their teen's emotional needs to understand and be supported in a shared dialogue. Being an authoritative parent requires time, knowledge and dedication. Authoritarian parents often interpret teens' sensitive emotions as weakness and try to suppress them with a quick defining comment – 'just do as I say' – or show who's boss by giving a slap or humiliating them. They act promptly and decisively and do not take the long-haul approach as the authoritative parent does.

Authoritative parents allow their teen to seek autonomy and independence. Instead of tight control, they closely monitor their teens' behaviour and correct them as needed. Authoritative parents also involve their teen in making decisions for the

family. Two-way communication is encouraged, whereas teenagers who grow up with authoritarian parents receive orders
instead of requests from their parents. Both authoritative and
authoritarian parents have high expectations of their teenagers;
they just approach them very differently.

I have seen a variation of this happening, though. Being
an authoritative parent sometimes requires so much energy
and time that parents give up holding on to the principles and
values they have, simply because they do not have the extra
resources it takes to live them to the fullest. They see themselves as authoritative in every sense, yet they are afraid of
being authorities. They seem so stressed and tired by everyday
chores that they simply do not have the energy to go into the
more long explanatory discussions, set rules constructively,
or meet their teen in daily briefings. They simply surrender
along the way. Therefore, a new kind of approach has arisen
where parents resign and thereby leave the responsibility,
and often decision-making, to their teen (and children) in a
misunderstood belief that 'I involve my child in the decisions
and give them co-determination, therefore I am a gentle and
authoritative parent'. It is simply misplaced goodness and
has nothing to do with being a tiger, lawnmower, or elephant
parent. It has come to my attention that some parents of this
generation may have such a hard time setting boundaries and
taking on a clear parental role that they show up in kindergarten with their still-undressed toddler wrapped in the blanket.
They hand the child to the teacher and let them put on their
clothes – they are exhausted these days, doing their very best
to make every day work.

It is a pity that some parents consider being an authority as wrong and harmful. It is essential to any child's well-being that they have something stable to lean on. Someone who can lead the way and exude security. What kind of world are we leaving to our children if even those who take care of them cannot show confidence in what they do? More and more children and young people struggle with uncertainty and anxiety. This might have something to do with the confusion around being an authoritative parent and not handling the ordinary chores of everyday life. A child or adolescent cannot carry the responsibility. We must secure a healthy and sound foundation for them to lean on and remember that at no stage in parenthood do we have control over our child, but we *always* have 100 per cent responsibility.

Your children are equal to you, but not with the same status, and that is the cardinal point. If you resign responsibility, you leave your child and teen insecure without someone to lean on. Rules and agreements can become a form of anarchy where everything is subject to debate and negotiations. Principles and values are loosened for the sake of peace in the family because there is no desire to go into discussions and quarrels.

Unfortunately, this backfires. You cannot be an authoritative parent without being clear and distinct in frameworks and values. The laissez-faire approach has had a renaissance, dressed in new clothes, that has produced a generation of bargaining adolescents who do not respect authorities and the boundaries of others because they have learnt that they must be involved in all decisions on an equal footing with their parents. It creates hurdles in schools and families because they have been taught that the world is about them and their needs, rather than being led by adults who know what is best for them most of the time.

To change the tendency of this 'me-oriented' new approach, you must take back the leadership role and trust that in the long run it makes a difference. Not in an authoritarian way, but by the hard work and dedication that an authoritative approach requires. There are no shortcuts; all there is to do is believe in the long-term effect without giving up along the way. I always illustrate this by saying that you have 100 per cent energy available during a day. How do you manage it? Spend 70 per cent on your work, 20 per cent on practical tasks, and have 10 per cent left, which must be distributed among your loved ones. Or how do the percentages look for you? It may be necessary to rearrange your day to make room for the energy needed to raise children and teenagers the authoritative way.

You strengthen what you practise. Suppose you want your teen to listen to what you say in mutual respect. In that case, you must be physically around them, present and available, and ready to show in action how good values and life are practised healthily. Someone might say that they do not have more time and energy than now, which I fully understand. However, when looking at how to prioritise, most people can find small pockets of unnecessarily wasted resources. Maybe it's OK to skip some chores sometimes if it means you're having a good time with your teen? Leave the laundry or lower your cleaning expectations and spend the time in the kitchen together or just go for a walk. There are many ways to 'clean up'. You show with your actions that you feel like spending time with your teen and that makes a difference. Remember, they already are what they want to become with their twinkling stars within. The parent–teenager relationship is a dynamic of equal respect and open-mindedness, which must always be nurtured.

Time-out versus time-in

'You are not allowed to drink alcohol', or 'If you don't respect me and the rules here in the house, go to your room and don't come out until you have learnt a lesson.' Ultimatums. Power struggles. Shaming or making your teen feel small teaches them that you are dominant and above them. You are not at eye level with each other, and you decide whether they are excluded with time-outs to think about their behaviour or allowed to be part of the activities in the family. I often hear time-outs being used to set an example. But there are simply no options to follow a time-out, and they are therefore much like ultimatums.

A time-out is a common method used by many to change the behaviour of their children and teens, and is generally considered a milder alternative to more severe reprimands.* The underlying intention of time-outs is to discourage bad behaviour by putting the teen in a tiresome situation they would rather avoid, such as sitting in their room for hours thinking about why they got drunk when they were not allowed to drink at all.

---

* In Denmark, spanking became illegal in 1997.

Teenagers behave incorrectly sometimes, and as parents, it is your job to guide them and not punish them for what they do not yet fully control. Sometimes you tend to operate under the assumption that your teen has control over their behaviour and intentionally breaks agreements and rules. This is not necessarily the case, and should it seem intentional, there is a wounded soul or unmet need behind the behaviour. Of course, it is essential to teach that certain actions are not OK. And this is where your role still matters and works well without ultimatums. Instead of being removed from a loving and comfortable environment, your teens need direction to identify their feelings and express them proactively instead of being isolated with their thoughts without the necessary tools to express themselves in better ways.

A time-in is a bit like a time-out but much more caring and valuable. It provides a break for teenagers to express themselves and calm down in a safe atmosphere, not threatened with ultimatums and being excluded. Having a parent present to co-regulate with the teen and provide language for their feelings, comfort and guidance on alternative methods of expressing themselves makes time-ins a better alternative for both parents and teens. If you only point out what your teen is not allowed to do, they will have difficulty figuring out what you want them to do. If you prefer keeping time-outs in your life, make sure to bring in time-ins to create a balance.

You and/or your teenager need to find peace and calm after the storm of a conflict. I know of families who have a 'sacred armchair' in their living room. Instead of being confined to your room, sitting alone with all your emotions, those who need it can willingly sit down in the armchair to have a moment on their own. No one may disturb them while they're sitting in the chair. It is a chair made for time-in. Anyone can take a turn for a while and not feel alone. I love this concept because we all need to be close to those who make us feel safe when calming our nervous system down. We find comfort in the fact that conflicts don't have to separate and create distance but rather invite inclusiveness, closeness and understanding.

I always react when someone does not treat people with respect or when an adult ignores a child's needs. Your teen mirrors you and you should bear this responsibility with tenderness, compassion and care. Make sure they understand your motives for acting as you do, to help them develop the skills to choose what feels right for them when building character.

Conflicts and no 'no's'

There is no doubt that adolescence offers many opportunities to escalate conflicts. The detachment phase is difficult for many to handle. Your pride may be especially hurt when everything you have put into the parenting role is compromised. You suddenly have to deal with feeling dispensable or ignored, that your opinions are no longer decisive, that alcohol is being consumed, and that agreements are not being kept. You try your best to encourage your teenager to respect your commands. You easily fall into the rut of talking about all that they are *not* allowed to do, but you are using your energy completely wrong.

Teenagers are unique when they receive 'good advice'.

Many don't hear the 'no's' in what you say to them. Because what you are basically doing is asking them to do what you don't want them to do. If you say, 'Do not drink alcohol', they interpret your words as an invitation even though you tell them not to drink. They will come home late when you say not to because they don't hear the 'no'. These 'no' phrases are interpreted as precisely the opposite of what you really want. What you should focus on, and what can help your teen and their brain development, is to change your language from can't-language to can-language.

So, instead of using 'no', an approach with positive connotations strengthens empowerment by focusing on what you can reinforce. 'If you are interested in drinking alcohol, let us find a way that works for all of us; I know we can do that.' 'See you at 10 p.m. – have a great evening.' 'I trust and love you.' This way of communicating makes it less complicated to collaborate with your teen if you want them to listen to what you are saying. Saying what you want from them shows them that you believe in them. It is a much more constructive dialogue for everyone and helps keep non-aggressive energy present. You must trust the upbringing you have practised and believe that they can largely figure out how to be, even if they live their lives differently than you would have chosen.

You cannot control the behaviour of your teen, but you can focus on strengthening your relationship. Sometimes, when there is turmoil in the family, there is a tendency to focus our worries on the teenager. But to get a realistic and truthful picture of the atmosphere in the family, it is advisable to look at the whole picture. Are there bumps in the relationship with your partner? Does work make you stressed? Do you interact from a place where your stars aren't shining and you are absent? Are you present and available for your teen? When parents call me to set up counselling with their teen, it turns out that many other things often are going on in the family. It can be illness, divorce, an affair, unemployment, relocation, etc., which affects the energy of the entire family. You find yourselves in chaos, targeting your teenager as the obvious focal point of your inner turbulence. This is not always the case, and therefore it's useful to think of the wider considerations when frustrations pile up. Of course, there will be times when your teen's behaviour is a problem, but always try to focus on not damaging the relationship too much.

Suppose you experience that your teen is lying and avoiding being with you. In that case, the reason can sometimes be found in a hostile atmosphere in the home. Imposing consequences on your teen is of no use unless the intention behind the lying or confrontations is clarified. Daring to be honest and vulnerable, you must feel safe to open up. If you are too preoccupied with your own emotions, you will not listen carefully, and so you cannot compromise or adjust any agreements with your teen.

The COVID pandemic is an excellent example of how it has been necessary to explain why it has been important to stay home and not go to parties with friends. We have all been taught to understand 'why' it has not been possible to do as usual but to behave with care and compassion for the benefit of the whole. The responsibility does not lie with your teen but with you because you are the one who ensures that they understand the motivations for their choices in life.

When using ultimatums, you communicate inequality and the use of control as core values. Whether you choose to correct, discipline, or empathise with your teen, you carry the responsibility of your actions and the messages they send. It is so easy to fall into the temptation of using ultimatums, but take a deep breath and remind yourself that you are still cultivating essential life lessons. Teenagers are supposed to push boundaries and test the rules. They are not full of bad or manipulative intentions; they are still learning, and this is good to remember when you are about to press the panic button and lose your temper. Remember, ultimatums and threatening language are powerful but not conducive to an atmosphere of closeness and trust. That is what must be in focus to bring up teenagers, always.

You need to keep tabs on your teens' lives and follow them as closely as when they were little. You must keep asking about their lives without giving advice. You must involve them and listen attentively, as you would with any other adult. Ultimatums are not something that you would use in discussions with your partner, mother, or neighbour. Therefore, you must stick to the authoritative approach with your teen, as it brings out the best collaboration.

Pyt

When you end up in a conflict with your teenager, it is hard not to take it personally if you are called a loser or other degrading things. If they close the door to their room to be alone or talk to friends, it may well feel like a rejection of you. In both cases, you are triggered and tend to respond with confrontation – 'This is not how you should speak to me.' Or you play the blame game: 'I thought the two of us were honest with each other. How come I'm not good enough any more?'

Sure, if you are called things that go beyond your limits, you must react. But this is best done by calmly approaching your teen once you have found your inner balance again. Once you have cooled off and understand the intention behind their behaviour, you can more easily let go of what triggers you and behave consciously. Not that it is easy. You tell them how it makes you feel to be talked to like that and that they probably wouldn't like it if someone called them a loser; that you have an agreement to speak appropriately to each other in the family, but also that you do understand their reaction if there was something that felt unfair. Ask them, *did* something feel unfair? That way, you don't make your teenager feel guilty but will set a limit on their behaviour without making a big deal out of it.

If you feel rejected in favour of your teens' friends, you must understand that they need to bond with someone their own age. Teenagers should not focus on having to be friends with adults. Therefore, you can practise not taking it personally, because your feelings have to do with your starry sky, not theirs. In fact, you seek a confrontation where they just do what they are programmed to do. Let them have some privacy and just accept it when your teens do not return or give you the attention you are looking for. It is OK that your teen is not coming to you any more, but that does not mean you should stop taking an interest in their lives. On the contrary, I meet many adolescents in my counselling who 'hate' their parents and have a complicated relationship with them. Those who feel most let down by their parents are those whose parents have interpreted their rejections as meaning 'leave me alone'. It is incredibly hurtful for them because behind this phase of finding themselves is your interest and persistence in wanting them; it is the way they feel loved and recognised. So never take rejection as an invitation to stop asking about their world!

In Denmark, we often use a word to move on from a situation that does not affect us too strongly emotionally. It may be when your teen has not vacuumed thoroughly enough and left some dirt on the floor. Or when they drank four beers instead of three at a party. It is a word that helps you move forward and not take everything too personally. The word is *pyt*, and it can best be translated as 'never mind'. Especially with children and teenagers, it can be helpful to learn that not everything has to be dramatic, even though the hormones swirl around in their system and call for big emotions. Sometimes it can be good to shrug and just say *pyt*. You can even buy a PYT button in numerous supermarkets in Denmark, and they are widely used in many families, kindergartens and schools.

The *pyt* word is *not* for undermining emotions or knowing how others feel. It is not to superficially say, 'It wasn't so bad, can't you just say *pyt*', or 'I don't think it hurts, go press the PYT button'. No, emotions must be taken seriously. Your teen must be able to be in a family or go to their school and have confidence that what they experience or feel can always be respected and believed.

The word *pyt* or a PYT button can be a helpful tool in situations where children and teens can handle smaller things themselves. Situations where they can say *pyt* and shrug their shoulders at lesser, insignificant things, such as if an assignment did not turn out as expected. If a pimple disturbs the 'perfect' look. When a voice breaks, or when sportswear is forgotten, or they've been given a difficult question, and so on. In other words, small everyday situations where they are not affected too emotionally but just need a way to get out of an awkward situation and move on.

Of course, decisions are always made on an individual basis. No one other than your teen can assess whether something belongs in the *pyt* category. Therefore, others cannot use the word or press a PYT button for anyone but themselves.

I like the use of *pyt* because conflicts are minimised, respect for the individual is strengthened, and there is generally greater inner attention to yourself and the well-being of others. You avoid ultimatums by being more gentle with what happens in the space between you and your teen. The Danish parents and institutions that use the *pyt* word or button recognise the difference that exists between learning to let things go while at the same time taking emotions seriously. Therefore, this word requires that you have a good sense of your own balance and that of the individual teen not turning any stars off.

CHAPTER 9

Freedom with Responsibility

DANISH ALCOHOL CULTURE

One, two, three, four beers. Nine, ten, eleven. A shot of vodka, and the party is ON!

The most anxiety-provoking development as a parent is when your teenager begins to show interest in drinking alcohol. Very quickly, all kinds of dangers appear for you, and your fear takes over. 'You are not allowed to drink alcohol!' 'It is dangerous.' 'You are going to behave stupidly.' 'Are you also going to smoke cannabis, then?' You hear yourselves list many horror scenarios that should make your teenager say to you, 'It's going to be OK, Mum. I don't want to get drunk; I just want to have a taste. I'll take care of myself, don't worry.' Few teenagers can honour that kind of reassurance, which is why they instead react to the mistrust that lies in such statements you place on them with rebellion. You give them your insecurity and fear to carry on their shoulders, which is the start of a relationship in freefall as your worries becomes their burden.

The truth is that underage drinking contributes to a range of acute consequences, such as injuries, sexual assaults, unwanted pregnancies, alcohol overdoses, and deaths. The bare sad fact is that alcohol consumption is a causal factor for more than 200 disease and injury conditions. Every month one teenager dies due to alcohol in Denmark, which unfortunately turns out not to be unique to us. On top of that, alcohol also affects the development of the brain – the part called the frontal lobes that are still developing and not fully formed until a person is in their early twenties. The frontal lobes regulate social competence, risk assessment and impulse control. One of the first effects of alcohol is that this particular part of the brain is anaesthetised. It lowers the teenager's already less-developed ability to assess risk, control impulses and, in general, show social competence, which explains walking in the middle of the road at night, drowning accidents, or falling asleep on railway tracks that may lead to some of the many negative experiences stressed above. Therefore, it is clear that you should worry about your teens taking steps towards conquering the world with a set of new party glasses, though you must not panic.

> Freedom with responsibility: to enjoy freedom, security and opportunity, you have to take responsibility for your actions. Every democracy begins with personal responsibility.

A civilisation of tipplers

Drinking alcohol is a matter of course for many in Denmark and a large part of the nation's social life on weekends, holidays and at parties. This was recently portrayed in Thomas Vinterberg's movie *Another Round*, a film which won Denmark an Academy Award for Best International Feature Film in 2020. It is about four high school teachers who want to test a theory that we are born with half a per mille too little alcohol in the blood, and is a moving insight into the Danes' joys and sorrows as a result of alcohol.

Join a Danish festival in summer, where music is important but the social community bonded with alcohol even more. Alcohol is served at birthdays, confirmations, town parties, private parent meetings, concerts and football games. You name it! Adults drink, adolecents drink. You will see teenagers gathering in playgrounds or in parks to socialise, play and drink with each other when the moon is up in the night sky. You will recognise them when they come singing in droves down the streets, laughing, kissing, arguing, or dancing to the latest hits – the seeds of young hearts sprouting like never before. As summer approaches, the annual celebration of passing high school certificates takes place with students dressed in white crowded into colourfully decorated trucks that drive them around to all their families and school friends, drunk and happy. At the same time, passers-by wave appreciatively at them from cars. We celebrate them and remember how it feels to be young, free of responsibilities, and extremely happy. Yep, almost everywhere where Danes meet alcohol is to be found. Enjoying alcohol is an integral part of our cultural identity; Danish children grow up exposed to it.

To be honest, enjoying alcohol is not something we are too worried about; well, intellectually on an abstract level, yes we are, but not when looking at our own habits. Quietly, we all know it would be a hurdle to socialise with our slightly reserved attitude if we didn't have alcohol's help to let our guard down and allow ourselves just to 'be'. We simply need a drink to be more open and relaxed. Going back to our ancestors – the Vikings – drinking has been the culture.

So, alcohol is so woven into everything we do, even though we are not alone in this. The total alcohol-per-capita consumption in the world's population over 15 years of age rose from 5.5 litres of pure alcohol in 2005 to 6.4 litres in 2016 and has remained pretty much the same since then. There are three World Health Organisation regions in which alcohol is consumed by more than half of the population – Europe, the Americas and the Western Pacific Region, and increasing numbers of drinkers are found in China.

Drinking facts and figures

Every Dane over the age of 18 bought an average of 9.5 litres of alcohol in 2019, which is close to the figure for Americans, who drink almost 9 litres and where there has been a change in cultural attitudes towards drinking especially among women, with stressed mothers referring to wine as 'mommy juice' and jokes about it being 'wine o'clock'. The British consume an average of 9.7 litres. In contrast, in China, the total alcohol consumption per person remained at 6.4 litres even though the numbers drinking are rising. The top spot is held by Belarus with total alcohol consumption of 14.4 litres. Yet

we are surprised that teenagers today drink as they do in so
many places, considering that non-drinkers make up nearly
half the world's adult population.

Looking at teenagers around the globe, more than a
quarter of all 15–19-year-olds are current drinkers, amount-
ing to 155 million adolescents. European countries top the
list of places where males drink in excess, starting with
Luxembourg, where an average of 4.4 drinks per day are
consumed by teenaged boys. Those teens are followed by
those in Denmark, with 3.8 drinks among males, in a country with the highest prevalence of drinkers among those top
10 countries, with more than 94 per cent of young people
consuming alcohol. The only country not in Europe in the
top 10 is Bermuda, where its male youth consume the same
amount as in Denmark. Although the Danish Health and
Medicines Authority's report from 2020 found that Danish
teenagers drink less than they did a few years ago, and even
though they start drinking later than previous generations,
they still drink a lot.

There is no doubt that high alcohol consumption carries
an increased risk that teenagers will have problems with
learning and education, and may develop a severe addiction
that they cannot solve themselves. It is difficult to argue that
Danish drinking culture can in any way be a role model for
others knowing that 3.8 per cent of Danish teenagers had
consumed such large amounts that they needed counselling
or treatment, according to the Danish Centre for Substance
Abuse. With the level of binge drinking, drunkenness, and
alcohol consumed, Danes have the highest levels of alcohol

consumption compared to young people in other European countries.

Binge drinking is defined as the intake of more than five drinks on isolated occasions, which increases the risk of alcohol-related illness and premature death.

Drinking obviously plays a significant role in teenagers' lives everywhere, as in Denmark. Up to 86 per cent of 15–25-year-old Danes drink alcohol because it is fun, while 38 per cent drink to not feel left out. Almost 54 per cent have experienced friends trying to get them to drink alcohol, even though they have said 'no thank you'.

There is a lot that determines how the alcohol trend will develop in the future. Living conditions, habits, time available, leisure activities, family background, friends and alcohol consumption patterns are significant. The same goes for the official alcohol policies where you live; economic factors and (social) media and advertising also have significance. There is a common notion and concern about whether declining alcohol consumption would be replaced with cannabis. Most young people who use cannabis also use alcohol, and the drugs are usually used simultaneously. However, cannabis use has not increased among teenagers, even though the attitude towards it is relatively tolerant as it is not perceived as anything special among most today.

Drugs

Whereas Danish teenagers drink a lot, it is more or less forbidden in other countries. If it is not banned, it is seen as being so harmful that other alternatives emerge and become the norm.

Marijuana is the most commonly used addictive drug after tobacco and alcohol in the US and its usage is at a historically high level among teenagers. More than 11.8 million use it. Among 10th graders, 28.8 per cent had used marijuana. In comparison, among 12th graders, it was 35.7 per cent, according to a 2020 Monitoring the Future (MTF) panel study. In the UK, marijuana is used by 18.7 per cent of 16–24-year-olds, while in Denmark the figure is 2 per cent of 15–25-year-olds. In the US, marijuana is fully legal in several states. It is perfectly normal to see teens walking around with a joint in their mouth or smell the characteristic odour in the streets first thing in the morning, and all day long. It is reasonable to contrast these figures and trends for the use of drugs and alcohol. I am not an expert in the field and can only convey the young people's alcohol intake in Denmark. However, there is some mismatch in how the health and well-being of young people are displayed. In Denmark, according to the Danish Medicines Agency, it is legal to buy and possess marijuana (CBD) as a consumer, but illegal to sell it as a retailer. You can therefore legally get medical cannabis in Denmark if your doctor has prescribed it and get the products delivered to a pharmacy. Otherwise it is illegal. In other countries, I have been told it is extremely easy to get marijuana, in the same way as it is for Danish teenagers to buy alcohol. I find that very interesting, for what is the balance of right and wrong?

I have never been into drugs and do not have a liberal attitude to narcotics. I am opposed to all forms; it is just not for me. To be honest, drugs terrify me and definitely awaken something within me that feels opposed to them. The thing is, I feel in my bones the pain of others hard and will instinctively try to remove all suffering from those who I sense have wounded souls. It is both a gift and a burden, but drugs awaken the holy Mother Teresa in me. That's not to say that everyone who takes drugs is a wounded soul, but through my work, that is what I have been tackling. My many years of work in psychiatry and with broken families and individuals have taught me that drugs can give rise to severe and devastating consequences. They cloud everything and have taken me deep into the darkest recesses of the soul where I have walked hand in hand beside those who have let me have a glimpse into their world. They had become addicted to narcotics in dark times. I embrace their pain and let them find reassurance that they are not alone on their journey to a better place, but I cannot bring the same kind of agony home. My home is my sanctuary; I need it to be kept free from too much pain. It is the only way I can embrace the complex and dark in my working life, without being weighed down too much by it in my private life.

My children know that drugs are unacceptable; they understand the consequenses they can leave and have full confidence in their father and me, which means they have not shown interest in them either. I am sure they know people who do use them, but I also know they will physically distance themselves from those on their path that use drugs consistently. Perhaps I am being two-faced when I let my girls drink alcohol while at the same time am quite harsh when it comes to drugs. However, I believe that they need to get to a place where they learn to find a balance – their limit – when it comes to alcohol intake. In contrast, through my work I have experienced that drugs often lead to addiction if consumed regularly.

Drugs and alcohol undoubtedly cause many worries when raising teenagers. The pain and powerlessness you might endure when unable to stop your teen being attracted towards a negative spiral can be tough. Every parent wants to support their teen whenever there is a need, even though it causes sorrow and many sleepless nights. I would like to emphasise that if your teen ends up addicted to drugs or alcohol, it is not always about your shadows, faded stars, or childhood trauma. Sometimes it just happens without being anyone's fault, and where it can be necessary to seek professional help. Remember this.

Your surroundings shape the 'normal'

Expectations and acceptance of a culture of alcohol consumption are crucial to how teens adopt it into their lives. It is important to stress that such norms are not created by parents alone. Norms are also made by society. Your surroundings form the framework around the lives of your children and teens. Therefore, the culture in which you live carries a responsibility around, e.g., how easily alcohol is to be found and at what age it becomes legal to purchase and/or consume.

I have always talked about how appropriate it is to drink with my daughters and have therefore, together with them, bought alcohol for them when needed. This is because ultimately it is my responsibility to prepare them as best I can to handle an evening drinking with friends. It is, however, an unequal challenge for you to try to postpone your teen's alcohol debut when society legalises alcohol at such an early age, making it available in every grocery store. Just like what happens in the home, where you have the responsibility to set a framework for how everyone in the family acts towards each other, setting what is acceptable or not, society has the same responsibility – only on a larger scale. In Denmark, the health authorities have just tightened the recommendations for alcohol so that its consumption is now discouraged until the age of 18, where it was previously discouraged until the age of 16. This is super positive.

Fortunately, more and more institutions and organisations make a great effort to slow down the alcohol culture of our still developing teenagers. When they were around 14 years old my daughters' school invited all parents to class meetings to state their non-alcohol policy. They knew from experience the challenges with alcohol that would arise and therefore wished that parents could be at the forefront and prepared to talk with their children before serious problems arose. The aim was for parents to collaborate on some guidelines for them and their teenagers to lean on collectively, postpone the start of teenage drinking, and create a non-alcoholic community around the class. Such an initiative was welcomed as some students had already started drinking on the weekends, while for others it was way out in the future. It was a fine and important endeavour, even though rules, tips and tricks can only be guidelines. Some follow them; others don't. In Danish high schools, colleges and other educational institutions, alcohol is allowed at school parties (not in junior high). If you are too drunk, the parents will be called, and you will be sent home, but moderate drunkenness is accepted. This is how the culture has been for many years, although more and more places are starting to offer alcohol-free events and parties.

Collecting memories

Community and *hygge* were never centred on alcohol in my family when I was a child. The adults enjoyed a cocktail before dinner on the weekend and a glass of good wine with the meal. There was no drunkenness, but enjoyment of alcohol in moderation along with the food that was conjured up in the kitchen. Good food with fine ingredients was always a priority, together with the presence of family members. I loved those family gatherings. However, I did party a lot with alcohol when I was a teenager in the late 1980s. I lived close to the sea, and all the local adolescents met on the beach on the weekends to be with their friends, party, and get tipsy. I was no exception; one night, there was a boy who poured beer into my hair – probably a mistaken way to get my attention – but my hair became so disgusting that I chose to use a beach washroom sink where the lights had gone out to wash it. When I woke up the next day, I could smell vomit, and wondered why. It turned out I had rinsed my hair in a clogged sink filled with vomit. Not forgetting another time when I locked my mother out one evening. I had had fun with my friends, I was drunk, and she came to shepherd me home. Actually, she brought our neighbour too, a family friend, and I got so angry that I ran home, went upstairs and lay down to sleep – but woke up suddenly recognising my mother's voice calling me from the other side of our front door. Embarrassing moments that were my itty-bitty youth rebellion, which created laughter later on.

In the same way, I know that my daughters also have a handful of fun and maybe embarrassing memories with them in the wake of the choices they make now. One thing that I have been very happy that my girls and their friends have done is that they have always danced at their parties. It is called 'floor' and both boys and girls spend a lot of time jumping around, playing air guitar and doing crazy cool moves. It is not about looking nice and perfect, but instead just to have fun with each other, drunk or not. Yes, memories are definitely present without alcohol, which is good to know – they are made by being physically present with friends when you are a teen. Even though I made mistakes, I still think I learnt to balance and find a healthy relationship with alcohol then. Today it is OK for me if alcohol is present, but it must not take precedence.

A culture in upheaval

I cannot deny that Danish teenagers drink a lot. I will not even try to convince you of the opposite; however, there is a growing understanding and acceptance that it is OK to say no to alcohol. Alcohol-free beers are on the rise – the minority sloooowly begins to become the majority. At least that is what I wish. A few years ago, you couldn't find alcohol-free beers, and now they are in every store, restaurant and bar with different flavours and different sizes. That is because adolescents of today are consciously choosing healthier paths as they are much more informed and purposefully work for personal and professional success. I even sense that there is an awareness today that it can be isolating to get very drunk. Instead of those who do not drink excluding themselves from the community, there is a developing tendency to exclude those who drink heavily instead.

My daughter Julie has never felt drawn to getting drunk. She has drunk some rounds but, basically, she thinks she can easily have fun without alcohol. She is confident and has strong social capabilities, and remains most often sober or just tipsy, rather than abstaining totally. Everyone knows she gives a lot to partying, even without alcohol. I find her strong and courageous in her willed solid choice, as she has become a role model for those ready to make a conscious decision themselves, not submitting to peer pressure while allowing her non-alcohol star to light up. I drink a glass of wine or champagne every now and then, but my eldest daughter drinks like most of her friends and sometimes behaves irresponsibly and over-indulges. My husband likes to drink an average amount of beer, and sometimes goes on weekend tours with his friends where they drink rather more. I would think we represent a fairly ordinary family with two almost grown-up adolescents.

Nordic studies have found statistical support for certain crucial factors behind the decline in alcohol use among teenagers. One is that parents tend to know more about where their teens are today and have greater control over what happens in their lives. They simply set more transparent rules on alcohol use than in the past. Of course, some parents do not have the energy and insight into their teenager's lives, as they have hoped. Still, in general, there is a greater focus on our teenagers today that supports this theory. Another factor is that teenagers today spend a lot of time in front of digital screens. There are only a few studies in the field, and therefore it cannot be said with certainty that this has an effect on teenagers drinking less. However, I have seen through my work that many adolescents who become addicted to gambling have a harder time socialising and, therefore, slowly change behaviour and, in the end, stop being social – at least when gaming has become an addiction. Conversely, social media can be used to access alcohol since, of course, there are always ways to reach consumers everywhere.

There may be a paradigm shift happening, where drunkenness slowly loses its function as a transition ritual between childhood and adulthood, as more and more teenagers reject that and instead pay attention to differences in lifestyle, gender and ethnicity to a greater degree than before. Many furthermore seem to value school and education and the notion of becoming happy and successful in life. They want to perform well, have close and meaningful friendships, and drink and smoke less. In our family, we have always taught our children that it is the close relationships and contact in everyday life that they must master. Not the connections that only exist when half a bottle of vodka is involved. It is crucial to look oneself in the eye, emphasise sober togetherness, have fun, and have a festive time without alcohol. That has been my goal in watching them grow up. When they started drinking alcohol, I knew they wouldn't do it to gain confidence in the social context but rather to discover this new phase in their life with the many new stars sparkling within them. They are not saints; they can party and be drunk, but they would be able to do exactly the same thing without drinking any alcohol, and I'm proud of that.

Finding a middle ground

Alcohol, and other temptations, will be a concern that will always exist when you have teenagers in the house. It is a period that you must look forward to instead of fearing. I remember that already when my children were small, I began to fear adolescence and the rebellions that I thought would follow. Luckily, my wise supervisor told me, as I aired my thoughts staring out the window, that it was an exciting time to rejoice in instead. It changed everything for me. I learnt the importance of reframing this period in my and my teens' lives to see the beautiful unfold: life as I have shown them, and watching them become wiser about themselves and who they are in a safe and secure environment. It has been my mantra since.

Trust is the keyword for me, together with a close and good relationship. No ultimatums. If there is something to focus on, I will always highlight these two things. Suppose your sky is filled with twinkling stars. In that case, you are more able to give your teen such an important foundation to enter adolescence. Imagine that your teenager comes home an hour later than agreed, that you get angry, blame and scold them. Of course, it may be necessary to refresh the framework of the agreements you have entered into. Still, in such a situation, it is good to remind yourself that their action is not intentional. Their worst crime will be that time ran out on them; they were amusing themselves or didn't want to leave the fun. And this is the cardinal point: agreements with responsibilities on how to cope with alcohol and playfulness are made jointly, where you as a parent have to compromise on something, and so must your teenager.

Rarely does your teen do anything deliberate to intimidate and hurt you, but they will challenge agreements you make when not including them. Agreements made jointly and unanimously make all the difference. It is all about involving them in decisions and finding a middle ground where both parties feel heard and met. You thereby avoid triggering some of your extinguished stars which tends to lead to ultimatums, but instead you polish your teenager's so that they shine a little more, which leads your teen to feel good and therefore want to co-operate with you. Win–win for everyone!

Therefore involve your teenager and agree on some terms that fit you both. Meet them with kindness and understanding if they unintentionally fail, so they feel that a good dialogue on how to do better next time is worth the chagrin. Keep in mind that their brains are still evolving, and even if they do their best, it may not be good enough in your eyes. Let them know that you trust them, understand their point of view and that you love the respect and trust the two of you share.

I want Denmark to find another leading place than to be one of the most drunk. At the same time, I am proud that we are one of the happiest countries in the world – and winning an Oscar was definitely great. There is a discrepancy here that needs to be addressed, and therefore I am glad that the trend among young people is reversing, so that alcohol consumption will hopefully fall in favour of everyone's well-being. Let us stand together for this change is needed worldwide.

CHAPTER 10

Empathy

REJECTION IS NOT OUR GREATEST FEAR – BEING INVISIBLE IS

One thing that has surprised me with adolescents is how I have had to redefine my parental identity as their detachment phase has grown in character. I always imagined that the way I have been a mother was something that I implicitly became in the split second I held my daughters in my arms. A noun that carried a fixed identity that I could hold on to the rest of my life. I was wrong, for pretty much everything I had practised as a mother – of closeness, physical contact, conversations about everything, shared cooking, night rituals, conflict management, diaper training, crying and laughter – now no longer felt of value. It felt like the last 17, 18, 19, 20 years of giving my daughters a good and healthy childhood were taken for granted, without endless credits in my pocket. I fell down the trap of self-pity. It was unbearable to view myself as 'invisible' as I *am* their mother! It is my identity, my heart, my life! But I had become a parent of older teens, ready to leave the nest, which felt frightening.

Empathy facilitates our connection to others. It develops in infancy through the relationship with our attachment figure. The more open you are to your own feelings, the more proficient you become at reading emotions.

The realisation of the need to redefine my parental role felt new and like treading water, because what was left then? I thought that the last years of adolescence were just a copy-and-paste of what I had practised the many previous years and absolutely not something that would require new skills and new revelations. Nope. The rules of the game were changed without anyone telling me. When I asked into my daughters' days, I was greeted by one-syllable words and no mutual interest in the conversation. Where once I had had their attention and dedication, now I suddenly felt a distance and absence of contact and began to grope blindly. What was going on with them? Why did they reject me? Did they have difficulties and didn't want to bother me? My thoughts revolved around them and what was going on to cause such a change. Was it my fault?

Same but different

Many parents struggle with these questions, and especially with being no longer needed in the same way as before. It is a con-tinuous battle within not to feel 'invisible' and then not take it personally. Rational thoughts and knowledge about this period take a back seat and many emotions of grief, frustration and anxiety show up. It hurts and causes distress when you quickly feel let down or not worthy of their consideration any more.

For me, it also opened up a new period of self-examination. My own starry sky came under the microscope again, and I realised that closeness and togetherness were associated with deep conversations with my own mother. That kind of bond, as I've explained earlier, was my mother's way of creating a connection with me when I was a teenager. I found that I might be repeating the same pattern with my girls. I unconsciously guided them through this form of contact that insisted on their nearness and reliable communication, defining their presence and closeness. As I became wiser about myself and how this new adolescent phase should be approached, the fear of my teens slipping out of my hands dominated my thoughts if I couldn't act as usual. Again and again, this phrase popped into my head:

It is about accepting that the premise of being a parent is different now. The premise of my mothering attitude is what I had to delve into. Here I had assumed I could expect the same from them as when they were younger while at the same time battling saying goodbye to the time I had given everything to. I found that I had to redefine my role. I thought the change I was searching for was not about me but about my daughters. Of course, I would always be their mother, but time now required me to focus more on acceptance than on how they withdrew from me or how they needed more privacy.

The sudden emptiness and sorrow of being replaced by

friends and young love was a feeling that I had to deal with without becoming bitter, or a reproachful mother. I had to find a way to make it work best, but I couldn't displace the inner turmoil that I felt. If what I had accumulated in all these years no longer works, then what was left? My daughters' dependence on me and the closeness we had shared daily was reduced to short intervals where I got a little dab of them. They did nothing wrong, for it is part of their natural development, but I had to find a new strategy that worked for me, even though there was no help to be found anywhere. I reversed my questioning and asked myself who was I and where did I go wrong? Was I too much, that made them distance themselves from me? But what I was searching for wasn't found in these questions, making me doubt myself. Instead, I had to interpret some new rules for the game, which I had no idea where to find.

A wave of pride

I first became more realistic and used my logic; I am dispensable for a while, yes – but they will come back one day. Right now, they have to fly and find themselves. They *must* break free. I know it. I knew that my daughters needed me just as much as when they were little, but in a new way. As soon as I realised this, I observed the fear disappear, and the light of joy, pride and confidence flooded me. I understood that my teens are just a new canvas on the wall that needs to be interpreted and analysed with curiosity and admiration. The same goes for your parental identity. Much is kept, but more colours are brought to the paper. One of the most critical prerequisites for teenagers to feel safe is clarity, and some fixed framework and routines to move in, which you can fulfil. It creates reassurance to know that the home is a safe place, with adults to trust and who let their starry sky sparkle as much as possible. These were my clues!

Focusing on the relationship is the first priority for me. It always has been. How could I forget that? But that was precisely because the relationship is changing and no longer the same. It must take a different form with teenagers and not be what the toddler experiences. Everyone, especially teenagers, is an equal and there needs to be a reciprocal relationship built on respect that is truly lived out. Like, when an adult speaks the same language to another adult.

It always makes sense to keep building on your relationship with your teen. Relationships need to be nurtured as they should in every respect, even when they move away from home, as my eldest daughter has. Gosh, it is hard. But the pride of watching her grow independently with autonomy and curiosity and enthusiasm in life makes my heart pound harder. Self-respect cannot even describe how great it is to feel her need to be 'I am the owner of myself' while actively choosing to have her sister, father and me in her life as well. She has become my adult child, and I approach her with a different attitude than earlier. Not less respectful, but more adult-like.

You must reinvent your parental identity to understand the dynamics at stake while always being the caregiver; having grown-up children can be scary. But look at it as turning into a mentor who cheers them on while they overcome the challenges and experience the bliss of the world on their own two feet, instead of being their go-to. Not a demotion, but an equally significant parental figure. Equality is important.

Hormone crash

Oh, 2020 was a challenging year. There was Covid-19 which caused many worries, cost lives and changed the circumstances of everyone in the whole world. While it was going on, I was working on my most demanding project ever. I developed a methodology for implementing the teaching of empathy in primary schools in Europe, made a complete tool kit (equivalent to a book), and held a five-day workshop – everything within half a year. It was insanely hard, and I was entirely alone on this journey. My oldest daughter travelled to Africa and worked as a volunteer for three months, facing new adventures there. At home, my youngest daughter struggled through college with remote learning.

I am conscientious, so, of course, I completed the project successfully, but I was exhausted like never before. My body felt apathetic, my period was absent, and I was just *so* tired, worn out by everyone and reacting to my beautiful teens from a place with absolutely no energy. I didn't use ultimatums, but I felt so sad to see myself hurting those who stood near me because I could not mobilise the strength to 'get up' and move on. Not fun.

Therefore, when the project was finished, I gave myself a few months where I was not allowed to work or start new projects and where I could put myself on pause for the first time in many years. My period continued to be absent. At the beginning of 2021, I went to the gynaecologist to determine if I might have reached menopause. Here, my doctor immediately congratulated me that menopause was over for me, which was a big shock. I had no idea I had been through it while everything else was going on as I didn't have any hot flushes. Still, my behaviour might be explained as a conglomeration of the stress and hormonal changes I'd gone through. I like to think of it this way. It feels more caring towards me, embracing myself with compassion and unconditional love in a tough time. Something I always strive to meet my daughters with when they slip.

I am not the only one hitting menopause while having teens. Honestly, that has not made my relationship with my daughters hard. Neither of them has rebelled very much, and they have, in fact, been very understanding of my 'busy' period. I have apologised for not meeting their needs when needed; everybody knew that I was out of energy. However, I know many who experience a major collision between them and their teens precisely because they are menopausal – there are two lots of rambling hormone zombies fighting for space where they can be seen and understood in the limbo they're going through!

The most common symptoms of menopause are hot flushes, difficulty sleeping and palpitations. There are also other symptoms associated with menopause and the altered hormone balance, and these include irritability, depression, concentration problems, fatigue, headaches and decreased desire for sex. And irritability, fatigue and headaches are an especially bad combo with a teenager who is constantly testing boundaries, which can cause clashes if you are not prepared for it. It is challenging to keep your head and deal with your teens' sour socks under the bed, dirty plates on chairs, and the smell of sweat that permeates the stagnant little teen room. 'You better clean up now! Otherwise, you won't be allowed to party tonight.' 'I have had a busy day and cannot bear to see you are lying in bed lazily. Get yourself a part-time job; otherwise, you will no longer get any pocket money.' Ultimatums creep out of you, and you know it is ridiculous because what is the next step? That they are thrown out of the house because you are gripped by something innately inevitable and lose sight of sanity? No, you are not going there. There is nothing to do but take the coincidence of two explosive hormone timebombs as a challenge to be tackled with your head held high. Suppose your relationship with your teenager is relatively intact. In that case, if you manage to listen to each other and not throw ultimatums around constantly, it need not be something you have to fear.

Go take in the world

Children become adults who make their own choices and make their own mistakes. They feel great trust from you when they experience the acceptance of their choices, especially when they are different from what you intended. Your adult teen is now in the process of practising this, for which they need space and freedom. I know of all the possible ways parents approach their adult teens. Some talk to their adult child several times on the phone every day, others less frequently. Some take over the daily chores which, with the best of intentions, undermines their adult child. Others do not listen when told no and override any attempt to show independence. You all find your own ways, and I don't have the right to say which works best. It is all a matter of who you are and what norms and traditions you carry with you. What matters is that how it is framed is an option that your adolescent decides to adopt.

Who among you can bear the burden of other people's choices? Not many, but that will happen if your teen does not learn to stand on their own two feet and manage themselves independently of you and without you steering them in a specific direction. Your teenager or adult child should not be a puppet ruled by you, as Pinocchio was by Geppetto, but hopefully be someone with a strong character who knows that they are responsible for their lives and their own well-being. You can still be an important background figure, remember.

Try letting them control the pace of visits or calls from home themselves. Most of my friends and I prefer to do it this way. Let them set the agenda. They need to feel that they are now in charge of their own lives and do not have parents who constantly rescue them. The moving-away phase that lies in handling a daily life is what your teen needs to learn. It gives them tremendous confidence to master adolescence, knowing that support can perpetually be found with you if required. When a rhythm has been found that works well, and as they initially dictate, when they reach out to you will be dictated by desire and not external expectations or guilt. That is what I feel is best and which works with Ida. Because I do not bother her constantly, she reaches out to me several times during the week and visits us occasionally. It is she who chooses and feels for what she needs, not us. A huge gift.

Turn on some stars

When the separation between parents and the teen who moves away from home goes smoothly, there is no disarray in the relationship. When you have a good connection, then that transformation will be optimal. To this end, it is good if you dare to look at your own starry sky. How much of it triggers you?

Understanding that you carry wounds and shadows from generation to generation is one of the most significant breakthroughs in my perception of parenting. I fully grasp the dynamics of putting your hurts onto your teen if you do not recognise them correctly. It can be painful and hard to delve into, so it is easier not to for many, but you will be better inclined to handle stress and bounce back better when needed. But grabbing just a tiny trim off a star is a step forward, and the outcome will teach you that it wasn't as terrifying as imagined. It is a healing process that will make a difference for your teenager and you.

I have been working on discovering my extinguished stars in my starry sky for a long time, and still today, I find small fragments that need my attention. My findings make me more thoughtful about myself and what I bring, but especially ensuring my girls receive a greater sense of acceptance makes me feel in balance. It provides more incredible energy and a more carefree start to your young adults. You get the life that you create. Ensuring that you have resolved any disagreements that would otherwise always exist between them and you before they move away from home provides better conditions for a sustainable relationship going forward. Remember that a child you know does not disappear because it leaves the nest. Life can change in a heartbeat, but why go and fear it. I have tread new steps from an unconscious belief that made me feel powerless into a more conscious one that finds this 'goodbye' transition empowering.

I am not invisible, and I don't want any anxiety to overtake me. I am more than happy that I couldn't figure out where my turmoil came from when my daughters were going to fly from the nest. It made me understand that even though you will always have an implicit identity as a parent, therein lies a dimension that I hadn't been aware of earlier. The detachment phase that allows your adolescent to be who they are, and you to be who you are, requires new thought and lots of empathy for yourselves. It is a struggle to recognise that what you used to build your kids throughout childhood you suddenly have to let go, and embrace that uncertainty is reality. You are still a parent, just in a new way that no one has explained before but paramount to a continued successful, close bond with your adult child. It is not a different game, but a deck of cards reshuffled and dealt out again.

Epilogue

A SUBTLE SENSE . . .

You are now aware that your upbringing contained barricades that can keep you from loving freely. It is true and so obvious that it becomes tragicomic that it isn't common knowledge. Think about how many of us could live freely and unleash our potential if we did not carry heavy baggage from previous generations on our shoulders. So much pain and hatred would not exist as it would have dissolved in the places from where they arose. Barricades usually turn out to be all the times we have not felt recognised and loved for who we are, which constitutes an unresolved remembrance of the past in certain areas that we will project out on the world to the ones nearest to us – our kids included. If we are not aware of these unconscious patterns, it will profoundly influence our children's well-being.

Many of us do not realise that our subconscious mind has great significance for the knowledge we can acquire about ourselves and thereby also on how we parent and are able to relate to our children.

It is easier to relate only to the conscious aspects of ourselves, as they are manageable and easier to point out. We do not give the subconscious aspects enough attention, although there are studies that show that the most significant activity in the psyche takes place outside the consciousness.

The subconscious mind is aware of everything all the time, in contrast to the conscious mind, which is unaware of everything that is going on in the subconscious mind. Only carefully selected information reaches the conscious level, whereas the subconscious acts as a video camera located in the corner of the room. It records everything that takes place, with no preferences or sorting, and the selection of what reaches the conscious level takes place here – and since our past is anchored in our subconscious self, our conscious thoughts and actions will be governed by the palette of emotions and memories that make up our entire self. In other words, we will always be *strongly* influenced by the good and bad experiences that we have with us from childhood. We will make choices that seem conscious but are distinctly rooted in the subconscious and camouflaged.

Being numbed out

Today, many parents want to transform their outdated and dusty parenting style into a more loving and wholehearted version. This comes from a subconscious feeling that something is not functioning optimally. There's a sense of subtle turmoil or dissatisfaction that isn't visible and therefore can't be pinpointed. It makes so many parents quite insecure and timid about their ability to raise their children as they wish, and they start looking for answers outside themselves:

'Maybe I should run a marathon; it will help me to feel better.'

'My children make me feel like a failure, which I always let them know.'

'I'm too busy at work, and we argue all the time at home. I think we need to change the scenery, to start all over again.'

'I hate myself when I'm not feeling good enough as a mother, which makes me unhappy. I will shut down all my social media channels, so I won't be reminded of how imperfect and incompetent I am.'

Unfortunately, the insecurity we bear without being able to clarify it or precisely narrow it down has affected our self-esteem and contributed to our high expectations for ourselves and our children. We are trying to control something we can't handle because it is invisible to the eye, but our children are sensitive and sense underlying emotions – and even though we do not think they perceive what is going on inside us, they do know. It is expressed in our tone of voice, the flicker of our eyes, red spots on the neck, shortness of breath, anger, sadness in the eyes, irony, sarcasm, etc., and they do grasp when we don't act from a place of inner peace. Our non-verbal or suppressed subconscious verbal way of communication will eventually reach them at some point, which indicates that there are issues to which we have to pay attention.

Nonetheless, we must understand that no one can live up to an unrealistically high level of perfectionism – and no one should because they will not have the heart and depth necessary to function optimally and live fully. We know that, but we don't know how to go about it. Author Joseph Campbell writes:

> People say that what we're all seeking is a meaning for life. I don't think that's what we're really seeking. I think that what we're seeking is an experience of being alive so that our life experiences on the purely physical level will reso-nate with our own deepest being and reality, so that we will actually be capable of feeling the rapture of being alive.

Nor should we change in favour of a momentary sense of satis-faction, for it is primarily about all the unspoken expectations rooted in our unconscious striving to feel valued and loved as we are. To change what isn't working, the arrow will need to be turned inwards in reflection for it to turn back outwards again in a healthier and more balanced manner – so that we learn how to connect the dots between combining the unconscious and the conscious. It does not have to be about turning everything upside down and going into therapy, but rather about creating an awareness of who we are and what we carry with us in life. The truth is that none of us has been 100 per cent fulfilled in all our needs as children. However, we are constantly altering our memories from the past so that they won't conflict with the present, and this awareness will apply to all of us. We therefore all bear some responsibility to ensure that our children do not end up carrying the burden of what actually is our job to work on, and this is exactly why self-awareness is so necessary and should be something we are all taught early on. If fear conquers the energising power and motivation of our longing, we will end up bitter and unhappy.

We pass the baton

Even before we become parents, most of us have some expectations as to how we envision a life with children. Some expectations for our kids belong to childhood norms and values of society, such as learning to walk after crawling, to being instructed at home and in kindergarten, school and professional environment, and learning how to operate socially. Being part of a society includes learning essential expectations, to be taught and practised with help from adults, otherwise it will be very difficult. But then there are also the expectations linked to our imagination, those that have appeared to us in our fantasies and our dreams, be it the pink children's room, the cradle, the adorable little soccer boots, the closeness and the connection to our offspring. Those expectations are the easiest for us to handle successfully as we can act upon them concretely.

The last set of expectations, however, belong to the unfulfilled needs that we have brought with us from our own upbringing. Things that haunt us and evoke all the unwelcome feelings like anger, frustration, hatred, disgust, bitterness, sorrow and anxiety. Those are unconscious and very challenging to picture because they bring up so many shameful feelings that go with them. And they are there, whether we acknowledge them or not.

As we haven't been taught how to recognise and acknowledge when expectations like these pop up unconsciously, we become experts on closing down emotionally. Our eyes darken, and no one can connect with us or feel our presence. From an even deeper place of sorrow within, we pass on our own unexpressed expectations to our children by forcing them to fulfil our broken dreams, or what has brought us pain. We point fingers at them for behaving badly, saying the wrong things, or causing this hopeless and meaningless situation that makes us feel uncomfortable. All unconsciously, of course, and if they do not just carry on the torch the way that we expect, then we accuse and blame them for not living up to *our* expectations, for not meeting the needs that weren't met within ourselves and which we are still hoping to fulfil.

We have all heard of the mother who never succeeded in becoming a professional dancer, and now, at any cost, her daughter has to fulfil the role of becoming the star in her class. Or the boy who cries every time he is on the soccer field, while his father yells at his son that real boys play football – and most certainly they do not cry. Very stereotypical examples, of course, but that is to highlight the image, as this happens all the time in different ways for everyone. All of us.

For instance, I did not sit the most well-regarded Danish matriculation exam – I chose a two-year programme instead of the classic three-year upper secondary education programme, and that programme was not the right one in my family. We have different options in Denmark, and our school system is put together differently than other countries, but the latter equates to a mix of high school and college. Therefore, it has been important to me that my children studied the 'right' programme so that they wouldn't be met with as little recognition as I experienced – because *that* did not feel good to *me* at the time when it was crucial for me to live up to parental expectations and acknowledgement to feel good enough in my family. I know my parents did not do it deliberately. Their way of letting me know was by talking a little condescendingly about the people who usually attended the same sort of school as mine. Those who did not have the same intellectual insight as those in the three-year school. It was not aimed at me, but in a way it was, indirectly. And, therefore, I did not feel good enough. This is just one example, rooted in experiences or unfulfilled needs that I experienced as a child, and which I was about to carry over on to my children, because my hurt feelings stayed with me and unconsciously affected how I wanted to advise my children in a specific direction.

Breaking down barriers

Turning around these unconscious patterns, it is much more meaningful to look for how they can benefit our children and ourselves. In my perspective, there are tons of learning opportunities and essential wisdom that should be common knowledge for everyone. It isn't easy, but it is a matter of practice and shifting a mindset from shame to honour to begin having a conversation about what is going on inside us. Showing more of our vulnerability with everything that this includes, good or bad, because that is what makes us able to relax and relate – not only survive – and thereby live fully.

As a parent, our kids will awaken the sides in us that we had shied away from because they were not welcome or benefitted us when we were children. They will eventually appear to us whether we choose to acknowledge these experiences or not. Children are better in the now. They are not concerned about the future or stuck in the past and yet are able to find some level of freedom within. They have access to something that we have forgotten or lost touch with. For example, I had not thought about how a part of me felt ashamed when I graduated, until my children chose their upper secondary education. Then it suddenly became clear that I wanted to direct them specifically by emphasising what is natural in such a choice, which I didn't wish to do intellectually as I knew that had to do with my past. I tried my very best to acknowledge and understand how I instinctively reacted, rather than responding in the best way possible: to understand my patterns of old hurt feelings, to make room for my daughters to choose from the heart and not from a place where they didn't want to disappoint me – two very different things.

Still, unfortunately, no one prepares us for the unconscious expectations of parenthood. And without us being aware of these processes, we continue to transfer old, outdated patterns and personal wounds from previous generations on to our children, without wanting to do so. We simply teach them that they can only be completely loved if they do as we wish for them to do and carry our old narratives and wounds together with us.

I have a deep wish and hope that soft values such as empathy and self-awareness will become an integrated part of teaching, and that we manage to break this harmful cycle in the school system one day. From a very young age, we create an awareness of who we are, and it should not only be the academic skills we become proficient in, but also learning those essential interpersonal skills that will help us build a healthier and more loving and peaceful world.

Gratitude fills my heart. This is the end of the book, and I have given you my best personal and professional tools to be best prepared for life with your teenager. I believe that if you do your best – nothing else can be expected – then everything will be fine. Do not doubt that inwardly, you know what means the most to you in life. Go for it!

Life with toddlers was hard and stressful, but also wonderful, meaningful and fun – while life with teenagers is a mix of self-reflection, healing of wounds, pride and gratitude. It is the stage when everything you have given to parenthood is rewarded. Where you, with sadness and admiration, can see your adolescent walking off up the country road like Hans Christian Andersen's steadfast tin soldier. Proud and upright and ready to conquer the world with all that it has to offer.

Life is amazing. Cherish the little moments with those you love. Having two young adults, I can say with certainty that I would give much to hold their small warm hands in mine for just a few seconds or sit next to them explaining body changes one more time. Time goes fast, and we often miss too many details in our hustle and bustle. Nothing in the world is bigger than the love of our children, and they will forever help us turn on our starry sky if we let them.

www.ibensandahl.com

Notes

For those who want more information or facts about my sources and references, you can find inspiration here.

Introduction

OECD (Organisation for Economic Co-operation and Development) study:
The OECD Better Life Index measures the well-being of different countries; www.OECD.org. The first World Happiness Report (http://www.earth. columbia.edu/articles /view/2960) was commissioned for the UN Conference on Happiness held in April 2012. It drew international attention as a landmark first survey of the state of global happiness. The World Happiness Report 2016 (http://unsdsn.org/resources/publications/world-happiness-report 2016/) found Denmark to have the happiest people.
And the repost from 2021 states that Denmark remains in the top three: https://worldpopulationreview.com/country-rankings/happiest-countries-in-the-world

Danes' genetic disposition for happiness:
https://warwick.ac.uk/fac/soc/economics/research/centres/cage/news/18-07-14-the_danish_happiness_gene/

The Danish Way of Parenting: What the Happiest People in the World Know About Raising Confident, Capable Kids by Jessica Alexander and Iben Dissing Sandahl (2014; Piatkus, 2016).

Chapter 1 Authenticity

Puberty:
https://www.sundhed.dk/borger/patienthaandbogen/boern/sygdomme/vaekst-og-udvikling/drenge-og-pubertet/
https://www.sundhed.dk/borger/patienthaandbogen/boern/om-boern/pubertet/piger-og-pubertet/

Mood Swings – the brain:
https://www.health.harvard.edu/mind-and-mood/the-adolescent-brain-beyond-raging-hormones
https://www.sciencenewsforstudents.org/article/hormone-affects-how-teens-brains-control-emotions

Percentage of conscious and unconscious thoughts:
http://webhome.auburn.edu/~mitrege/ENGL2210/USNWR-mind.html

The 90 second rule:
https://care-clinics.com/did-you-know-that-most-emotions-last-90-seconds/

How many thoughts do we think in a day?
https://www.mvorganizing.org/what-percentage-of-our-thoughts-are-unconscious/#How_many_thoughts_do_we_think_in_a_day

6,000 thoughts a day:
https://www.newsweek.com/humans-6000-thoughts-every-day-1517963

How to measure a thought:
https://videnskab.dk/krop-sundhed/hvor-mange-tanker-kan-hjernen-taenke-paa-samme-tid

Cornell University study:
https://tlexinstitute.com/how-to-effortlessly-have-more-positive-thoughts/

Negative thoughts:
https://www.nature.com/articles/s41467-020-17255-9

Mark Twain:
https://en.wikipedia.org/wiki/Mark_Twain

Fight, flight, or freeze is an automatic physiological reaction:
https://en.wikipedia.org/wiki/Fight-or-flight_response

The fawn response:
https://www.psychologytoday.com/us/blog/addiction-and-recovery/202008/understanding-fight-flight-freeze-and-the-fawn-response

Chapter 2 Reframing

Debbie Ford:
The Shadow Effect by Deepak Chopra, Debbie Ford and Marianne Williamson
(HarperCollins, 2010).
https://debbieford.com/
http://thefordinstitute.com/shadow-work

Shadows in psychology:
https://en.wikipedia.org/wiki/Shadow_(psychology)
https://medium.com/big-self-society/shadow-work-a-simple-guide-to-transcending-the-darker-aspects-of-the-self-e948ee285723

Carl Gustav Jung:
https://da.wikipedia.org/wiki/Carl_Gustav_Jung

Chapter 3 Trust

Trust definition:
https://da.wikipedia.org/wiki/Tillid
Tillid by Gert Tinggaard Svendsen (Tænkepauser, 2012).

K. E. Løgstrup:
https://www.kristeligt-dagblad.dk/liv-sj%C3%A6l/i-begyndelsen-er-tilliden

Former Danish prime minister:
https://da.wikipedia.org/wiki/Poul_Nyrup_Rasmussen

Danish mother in New York, 1997:
https://www.theguardian.com/us-news/2017/nov/26/anette-sorenson-denmark-new-york-baby-left-outside

The Pygmalion effect:
https://thedecisionlab.com/biases/the-pygmalion-effect/

Chapter 4 Play

Lev Vygotsky:
https://en.wikipedia.org/wiki/Lev_Vygotsky

Learning by doing:
https://en.wikipedia.org/wiki/Learning-by-doing

Percentage of Danes with access to the internet:
https://www.dst.dk/Site/Dst/Udgivelser/GetPubFile.aspx?id=29450&sid=itbef2020

US percentage of internet access:
https://www.statista.com/statistics/183614/
us-households-with-broadband-internet-access-since-2009/
In the United Kingdom 94.62 percent of the population were using the
internet in 2020.
https://www.statista.com/statistics/468663/uk-internet-penetration/

Mobile phone access:
Denmark – https://mobilabonnement.dk/guides/
hvad-er-dit-mobilforbrug-sammenlignet-med-danskernes
US – https://www.pewresearch.org/internet/fact-sheet/mobile/
79 million mobile phone subscriptions are registered in the UK
https://www.statista.com/statistics/468674/
mobile-cellular-subscriptions-in-uk/
China and India – https://worldpopulationreview.com/country-rankings/
cell-phones-by-country

Phone addiction:
In 2022 – https://www.reviews.org/mobile/cell-phone-addiction/
US – https://www.commonsensemedia.org/the-new-normal-infographic
Danish – https://ifsv.ku.dk/nyheder/
mobilafhaengighed-er-relateret-til-daarligt-helbred/
UK addiction: https://www.slicktext.com/blog/2019/10/
smartphone-addiction-statistics/

Teenagers' average use of phones:
Danish – https://www.gjensidige.dk/familien/teenliv/den-digitale-teenager
American – https://www.commonsensemedia.org/sites/default/files/uploads/
research/2019-census-8-to-18-full-report-updated.pdf

Insight Manager report:
https://www.businessofapps.com/data/tik-tok-statistics/

Billion TikTok users:
https://www.commonsensemedia.org/sites/default/files/research/
report/2019-census-8-to-18-full-report-updated.pdf

Danish teenagers spend less time with friends physically:
https://www.sdu.dk/da/sif/ugens_tal/11_2016
https://www.boerneraadet.dk/media/75093/BRD_Pixi_Unge_og_
medier.pdf

Gaming addiction:
Do You Want to Raise Happy Children? Parent The Danish Way. Online
course, 2019.

Chapter 5 Formation

Forty per cent of Danish students attend an *Efterskole*:
https://via.ritzau.dk/pressemeddelelse/rekordstor-andel-tager-efterskole-i-10-
klasse-isaer-andelen-blandt-unge-med-foraeldre-med-relativt-hoje-indkomster-
er-stigende?publisherId=3274962&releaseId=13599285

The educational ideas of Grundtvig:
'People learn by talking with each other.' https://www.efterskolerne.dk/

The word *efterskole* translates to 'after school':
https://issuu.com/efterskoleforeningen/docs/dannelse_that_works_web

The historical and cultural origin of the *efterskole*:
https://www.efterskolerne.dk/Faglig_viden/
Efterskolens_historie_og_vaerdigrundlag
https://www.efterskolerne.dk/English/educationalideas

Formation:
https://frivillighed.dk/files/media/documents/frivilligrapporter/
handout_1_-_folkemoedet_2019_1.pdf
https://frivillighed.dk/guides/6-faktorer-der-motiverer-og-fastholder-frivillige

The Danish welfare society:
https://undervisning.deo.dk/gymnasium/danske-vaerdier-i-europa/
velfaerdssamfundet/

Mr Oh:
https://en.wikipedia.org/wiki/OhmyNews
http://www.ohmynews.com/

The N. F. S. Grundtvig Prize:
https://www.altinget.dk/civilsamfund/navnenyt/
grundtvigs-pris-2018-gaar-til-sydkoreansk-journalist

Chapter 6 Togetherness

Nonverbal communication:
https://www.pgi.com/blog/2020/03/
how-much-of-communication-is-really-nonverbal/

How friendship networks give better mental health:
https://srcd.onlinelibrary.wiley.com/doi/abs/10.1111/cdev.12905
https://www.newportacademy.com/resources/empowering-teens/
teen-friendships/

How social rejection feels like physical pain:
https://news.umich.edu/study-illuminates-the-pain-of-social-rejection/

Daniel J. Siegel:
https://greatergood.berkeley.edu/article/item/
how_the_teen_brain_transforms_relationships

Darwin:
https://da.wikipedia.org/wiki/Survival_of_the_fittest

Özlem Cekic:
https://www.ozlem.dk

***The Five Love Languages* by Gary Chapman:**
https://www.5lovelanguages.com/

Helen Fisher study:
https://pubmed.ncbi.nlm.nih.gov/16255001/
https://hms.harvard.edu/news-events/publications-archive/brain/love-brain

How love is addictive:
https://www.experimentarium.dk/psykologi/
forelskelse-kommer-naar-det-er-foraar/
https://www.sexogsamfund.dk/sites/default/files/foldertilforaeldre-7-
10klassetrin_2.pdf
https://www.sexogsamfund.dk/sites/default/files/foldertilforaeldre-4-
6klassetrin_1_0.pdf
https://www.sexogsamfund.dk/sites/default/files/20170522_sex_og_
samfund_mokka_a4_300_dpi.pdf

Chapter 7 Uniqueness

Erik H. Erikson:
https://www.ncbi.nlm.nih.gov/books/NBK556096/
https://michaelhusen.dk/personlig-og-social-identitet/

'Identity', word origins:
https://www.dictionary.com/browse/identity

American Society of Plastic and Reconstructive Surgeons, report:
https://www.plasticsurgery.org/documents/News/Statistics/2020/plastic-
surgery-statistics-full-report-2020.pdf
https://www.isaps.org/wp-content/uploads/2019/12/ISAPS-Global-Survey-
Results-2018-new.pdf

Danish plastic surgeons on the change:
https://heartbeats.dk/unge-under-kniven-for-at-ligne-deres-selfies/

Body Dysmorphic Syndrome (BDS):
https://www.forbes.com/sites/annahaines/2021/04/27/
from-instagram-face-to-snapchat-dysmorphia-how-beauty-filters-are-
changing-the-way-we-see-ourselves/?sh=66b1c8604eff

Breasts grow until the age of 21:
https://teens.webmd.com/teens-plastic-surgery

Céline Brassart Olsen:
https://motheringinthenow.com/

Gender directions:
https://www.zetland.dk/historie/sOJvGXwv-aOPVJMB3-790c1

WHO broad definition of sexuality:
https://www.who.int/health-topics/sexual-health#tab=tab_1
https://vidensportal.dk/temaer/seksuelle-overgreb/borns-seksuelle-udvikling

The five sex languages by Jaiya:
https://missjaiya.com
https://orionsmethod.com/podcast/
jaiya-discover-your-desires-through-your-sexual-blueprint/

The number of young people who have bought prescription potency drugs:
https://www.tv2ostjylland.dk/oestjylland/
kaempe-stigning-saa-mange-unge-bruger-nu-viagra

Chapter 8 No ultimatums

The United Nations Convention on the Rights of the Child:
https://www.ohchr.org/en/professionalinterest/pages/crc.aspx

Authoritative and authoritarian parents:
https://www.psychologytoday.com/us/blog/thinking-about-kids/201409/
authoritative-versus-authoritarian-parenting-style
https://en.wikipedia.org/wiki/Parenting_styles

Time-out versus time-in:
https://time.com/5700473/time-outs-science/
https://www.ahaparenting.com/read/timeouts

Spanking illegal in Denmark:
https://en.wikipedia.org/wiki/Child_corporal_punishment_laws
https://faktalink.dk/titelliste/revs

Can't-language and can-language:
https://hjernesmart.dk/

The *pyt* word:
https://videnskab.dk/kultur-samfund/sig-pyt-og-forebyg-stress

Chapter 9 Freedom with responsibility

Alcohol a causal factor for disease and injury:
https://www.who.int/news-room/fact-sheets/detail/alcohol

Freedom with responsibility:
https://www.folkeskolen.dk/13281/frihed-under-ansvar
http://www.skoleborn.dk/maj_2018/07-saadan-opdrager-foraeldre.html

The total alcohol per capita consumption in the world's population over 15:
https://apps.who.int/iris/bitstream/handle/10665/274603/978924156563
9-eng.pdf?ua=1

The three WHO regions in which alcohol is consumed by more than half of the population: the European region (59.9 per cent of current drinkers), the region of the Americas (54.1 per cent), and the Western Pacific Region (53.8 per cent):
https://apps.who.int/iris/bitstream/handle/10665/27460
3/9789241565639-eng.pdf

Every Dane over the age of 18 bought an average of 9.5 litres of alcohol in 2019:
https://www.dst.dk/da/Statistik/nyt/NytHtml?cid=30798

'Wine o'clock'
https://www.foxbusiness.com/lifestyle/alcohol-consumption-increase-in-us

Total alcohol consumption:
Britain – https://www.thedrinksbusiness.com/2019/11/
the-average-brit-drinks-108-bottles-of-wine-a-year/
China – https://www.frontiersin.org/articles/10.3389/fpsyt.2020.597826/full
Belarus – https://worldpopulationreview.com/country-rankings/
alcohol-consumption-by-country

Current drinkers among adolescents in the world:
https://apps.who.int/iris/bitstream/handle/10665/274603/978924156563
9-eng.pdf?ua=1

Bermudans consume the same amount as Danes:
https://www.usnews.com/news/best-countries/articles/2018-09-20/
drinking-extremes-where-the-worlds-youngest-and-oldest-imbibe-most

Danish Health and Medicines Authority's report from 2020:
https://www.sst.dk/-/media/Udgivelser/2020/ESPAD/ESPAD.
ashx?la=da&hash=F3FB3235794E1FDE180FB3D4B0FC23333A6BF765

Danish Centre for Substance Abuse:
The questions come from AUDIT (The Alcohol Use Disorder Identification

Test), one of the most widespread screening instruments for identifying and assessing alcohol problems, according to the Danish Society for General Medicine.

According to results from ESPAD, the European School Survey Project on Alcohol and Other Drugs, who reported alcohol use in the last 30 days, Danish studdents drank alcohol on 5.6 occasions on average. Students from Germany and Cyprus consumed alcohol on 8.0 and 7.5 occasions, respectively, and students from Sweden, Finland, Lithuania, Iceland, Estonia, Latvia and Norway drank alcohol on fewer than 4 occasions on average. In most countries, boys who drank in the last month did so more frequently than girls, with a difference of more than three occasions in Germany, Serbia and Montenegro. One in three students (34 per cent) reported heavy episodic drinking (five or more glasses of alcoholic beverages on one occasion at least once in the past month). This drinking pattern was found more often in Denmark, Germany and Austria. It was reported by between 49 per cent and 59 per cent of students. The lowest figures were found in Iceland (7.6 per cent), followed by Kosovo (14 per cent) and Norway (16 per cent).

ESPAD: The report is based primarily on the information provided in 2019 by 99,647 students from 35 European countries, 25 of them being Member States of the European Union. Nearly 700,000 students have participated in the seven successive ESPAD data-collection waves, making the project the most extensive harmonised data collection on substance use and risk behaviours in Europe. The ESPAD database is also available to researchers outside the ESPAD network, who may apply for access. https://www.emcdda.europa.eu/system/files/ publications/13398/2020.3878_EN_04.pdf

Binge drinking:
https://alkohologsamfund.dk/alkopedia/fakta-om-unge-og-alkohol

The economic factors and (social) media and advertising significance:
https://nordicwelfare.org/wp-content/uploads/2019/03/ What%E2%80%99s-new-about-adolescent-drinking-in-the-Nordic- countries_FINAL.pdf

Marijuana the most commonly used addictive drug after tobacco and alcohol in the US:
https://www.drugabuse.gov/news-events/news-releases/2021/09/ marijuana-use-at-historic-high-among-college-aged-adults-in-2020

2020 Monitoring the Future (MTF) panel study:
https://www.drugabuse.gov/drug-topics/trends-statistics/monitoring-future

Marijuana use in Denmark corresponds to 2 per cent:
https://socialstyrelsen.dk/nyheder/2019/move-
effektiv-behandling-af-unges-rusmiddelprobleme/
om-unge-der-har-et-misbrug

Nordic studies:
https://nordicwelfare.org/wp-content/uploads/2019/03/
What%E2%80%99s-new-about-adolescent-drinking-in-the-Nordic-
countries_FINAL.pdf

Screentime and drinking:
https://nordicwelfare.org/wp-content/uploads/2019/03/
What%E2%80%99s-new-about-adolescent-drinking-in-the-Nordic-
countries_FINAL.pdf
https://www.information.dk/debat/2021/01/
danske-drukkultur-hylder-stangstive-fulderik
https://www.emcdda.europa.eu/system/files/
publications/13398/2020.3878_EN_04.pdf
https://www.berlingske.dk/aok/
dansk-alkoholkultur-er-ikke-som-i-andre-lande-min-generation-var-den-foerste
https://www.sst.dk/~/media/5F28779EEB03442585F1CB199119BEF5.ashx

Chapter 10 Empathy

Menopause:
https://www.sundhed.dk/borger/patienthaandbogen/kvindesygdomme/
sygdomme/hormonbehandling/overgangsalderen/
https://netdoktor.dk/sunderaad/fakta/overgangsalder/symptomer_i_
overgangsalder.htm

Letting go:
https://sund-forskning.dk/artikler/hjernen-kan-laere-at-give-slip-pa-traumer/
Anita Moorjani, Dying to Be Me, https://www.anitamoorjani.com/

Epilogue

There are studies that show that the most significant activity in the psyche takes place outside your consciousness:
Derfor forelsker du dig aldrig i den forkerte by Jytte Vikkelsøe (Gyldendal, 2017).

Your childhood experiences are camouflaged and rooted in the unconscious:
The Self-Aware Universe by Amit Goswami (Tarcher, 1993).
The Power of Myth by Joseph Campbell (Doubleday, 1988).

Index